# A SHORT COMPARATIVE
# HISTORY OF RELIGIONS

BY

THEODORE H. ROBINSON,
Litt.D., D.D., D.Th.

SOMETIME PROFESSOR OF SEMITIC LANGUAGES, UNIVERSITY
COLLEGE, CARDIFF

GERALD DUCKWORTH & CO. LTD.
3 *Henrietta Street, London, W.C.* 2

# PREFACE

LET us imagine that on a lofty hill-top, overlooking the surrounding country, there stands a vast prison. It is so arranged that every cell has a window, from which the occupant can look out on the world and form opinions and judgements on it. No two of the windows give exactly the same view. Some are large, some are small; some look only towards the sky, others are directed to the earth alone; some are covered with tinted glass and some with deeper colours. But none shows the outside in perfectly clear sunlight, and, with all their differences of character and range, none gives more than a partial view of the world in which the prison is set. And it is only when the prisoner is liberated that he is able to form any final estimate of that world, and to know how far his cell window has admitted him to a knowledge of the Truth.

The student of religion is sometimes impelled to feel that men in their quest of God are in much the same case as the prisoners of our parable. None can justly claim an absolute and final understanding of all that can be known of God. Even if a religion can be said to hold within itself all truth, most of it must remain hidden from individuals, and only patient research within the limits of a particular religion will advance its adherents in knowledge and appreciation. A Christian may—probably must—hold Jesus to be the final and complete revelation of God, but only the most arrogant Christian would claim that he knew all there was to be known about Jesus. For ages man has been struggling towards God, and in this twentieth century we yet stand, as it seems, far nearer to the beginning of the quest than to the end. Our records do not carry us back for more than seven thousand years, and if the conscious search for God began twice as many years ago, we may well ask, What are fourteen thousand years as compared with the period during which it seems possible that man may yet endure as a physical species upon this material earth?

Whatever form, then, the world's final religion may take, it is worth while studying its history up to the present. For we can see how religions are born, develop, and die. The dead religions are more numerous than the living, and they have died, not so much because they have been killed by outside forces, but because they have contained within themselves the seeds of decay. A religion, if it is to live, must have the power of approximating towards an ideal which no man consciously sets before himself, but to which he is, none the less, definitely moving. It must be able to adapt itself to the whole of human nature, and to the changing needs of successive generations; above all, it must maintain within itself a real spiritual vitality.

I have therefore endeavoured to use the more important of the historic religions of the world as illustrations of general tendencies, to treat of each with impartiality, and to confine myself, as far as possible, to the plainest statements of fact. I confess that I cannot hope to claim success, and I fear that I may, after all, have failed most completely where I would most have wished to succeed. For it seems to me that Christianity itself can only be rightly appreciated when it is set alongside of the world's other faiths, and treated with exactly the same detachment and from precisely the same external standpoint as the rest. I have little doubt, then, that whilst some readers will find what I have to say about Christianity too cold and unsympathetic, there are others who will feel that it

receives undue preference. Yet, save in one particular, I
have tried to avoid making contrasts, believing that the
plain facts are in themselves sufficient.

In the nature of the case no one man is competent to
speak of the whole field. It is not enough merely to have
read books about a religion, or even to have studied its
literature, if it have a literature; for full appreciation it is
necessary to have spent many years in close and intimate
contact with people who profess the faith under observation, to have seen its highest, its lowest, and its typical
forms, and to have practical observation of the place it
holds in man's life and thought. Even such study as this
is inadequate unless there be a real power of sympathy,
the capacity for entering into the very mind and soul of
another, to see life and faith as he sees them—a gift
bestowed on few men. A whole lifetime is all too short for
the understanding of any one religion. I can claim some
acquaintance with the literature of Judaism, Islam, and
Hinduism (the last almost entirely through translations),
and I have seen both Hinduism and Islam at work, but
the section on Judiasm is the only one in which I have
ventured to rely solely on my own judgement. I have very
gratefully to acknowledge the kind and willing help of
distinguished students of different religions, who have
looked over the sketches I have drawn and made important suggestions. Thus Dr. W. O. E. Oesterley has been
through the first three chapters, and Dr. Sidney Cave the
first six. My colleague, Professor Gilbert Norwood, has
read the paragraphs which touch on the Græco-Roman
world, Dr. Kenneth Saunders the portion which deals
with Buddhism, Professor Percy J. Bruce the different
sections which allude to Chinese religion (apart from
Buddhism), and Professor A. Guillaume the chapter on
Islam. I am indebted to several friends, amongst whom I
must especially mention Canon D. C. Simpson, Oriel
Professor at Oxford, for valuable advice and help in

preparing the last chapter. Finally, the Rev. B. Grey Griffith of Cardiff has been good enough to go through the whole and call my attention to many slips, blunders, and infelicities in expression. Whilst the general plan and the scope of this little volume have made it impossible for me to use the expert knowledge that each of these gentlemen possesses in his own sphere of study to the extent that I should have wished, I believe that their advice has preserved us from serious errors alike of fact and of emphasis.

Lastly, I may express the hope that I may succeed in sending readers of the following pages to a fuller study, not only of the separate religions, but of the general subject—the growing power of man to appreciate God and to commune with Him.

THEODORE H. ROBINSON.

CARDIFF.
*September, 1925.*

# PREFACE TO THE SECOND EDITION

THE issue of a new edition has made it possible slightly to modify a few passages, where the progress of thought seems to make additions or changes most desirable. These occur for the most part in the earlier chapters, since the main facts of the great historic religions naturally undergo little change in a few years. A Bibliography has been added, including a small selection of books which may be useful to the beginner.

It is with very great pleasure that I express my thanks to Dr. N. Micklem of Mansfield College, Oxford, who has allowed me to consult him as to the changes I have made, and to the Rev. E. A. Payne, who has given invaluable help and advice on the Bibliography. My wife, too, has again rendered that service which she has so constantly given me during the last thirty years, and read the proofs with me.

In conclusion I can only hope that this little volume may play its part in Christian thinking by introducing its readers to a subject whose importance is more fully recognized to-day than ever before. The true greatness of Christ begins to dawn on us only when we have seen something of the way in which other faiths have ministered to the human spirit.

THEODORE H. ROBINSON.

EALING.
*May*, 1950.

# CONTENTS

# A SHORT COMPARATIVE HISTORY
## OF RELIGIONS

### I.—INTRODUCTORY

RELIGION is one of those terms which baffle logical definition. The attempt has been made again and again, and no
definition ever offered has both covered the whole field
and excluded everything else. Nevertheless, there are few
of us who do not understand what we mean when we
speak of religion, and some of us are prepared to recognize
that it is something so fundamental that definition is as
unnecessary as it is impossible. Most of us would be hard
put to it to define life, but few of us would fail to distinguish between the living and the dead.

Religions are living entities, and we may therefore
compare and classify their different forms as we compare
and classify other living things, without ultimate definition. In other words, the study of religions is in a certain
sense a kind of biology. There is, so to speak, an "evolution" of religions, and a "phylogeny." There are "normal"
types, there are extinct species—often of importance in
determining the actual history—and there are "freaks."
But the study of religions differs in one or two serious
aspects from that of physical biology. The material on
which we have to work is much more elusive, and its
interpretation is much less certain. The "ancillary
sciences," of which the two most important are psychology
and archæology, are still in their infancy, and there are,

1

therefore, wide differences of opinion as to the correct explanation of a number of the phenomena, especially in the "lower" forms. We are faced, moreover, with at least one fact which the physical biologist can afford to ignore. This is "hybridism," which in the material world leads no farther down the evolutionary path, and can be neglected, since it is concerned with isolated individuals and not with the great mass of types. But in religion the analogous phenomenon, commonly known as "syncretism," is of very frequent occurrence, so frequent that we may doubt whether any of the "higher" religions exists to-day in a pure form or ever has so existed since the days of its founder. It is true that there is a constant effort to get back to the original essence, and that even in those religions that have suffered most the ideal is not wholly lost. But as the various religions come before the observer, he has to note and account for the phenomena as they are, even though in his own mind there may be a clear conception of the primary purpose of the founder and of the ultimate form which it will take.

The features presented by the various religions of the world can usually be grouped under three heads. The first of these is *Theology*. This is, strictly speaking, the view, theory, or opinion which the worshipper holds about the object of his worship. It would not be accurate to say the view held of God, for in many religions it can hardly be said that there is any real conception of deity at all. When we speak of God, or even of a god, though perhaps no two of us would give exactly the same definition of what the terms meant to us, we should all agree that they implied definite and distinct personalities. A religion which recognizes the existence of only one God obviously does this; but even where there are many gods, each of them is held to have a certain distinctiveness and an individuality of his (or her) own. In some of the most primitive and in some of the most advanced forms of religion there is no object of worship of which this can be said. On the one hand there are forms of creed in which the spiritual beings with whom man believes himself to come into contact are not clearly separated one from another. They have no individual names and no independent personality, but merely form groups, even if they are differentiated to this extent. In other religions, on a far higher plane of intellectual development, all idea of a personal deity has been transcended by a philosophy which declares that individual personality, human or divine, is either temporary or unreal, and that there is only a single universal entity, of which all phenomena are parts. In these circumstances it is impossible that there should be any personal object of worship—or, strictly speaking, any worship at all. Nevertheless, the religion which claims to-day more adherents than any other is theoretically of this type, though in practice most of its forms recognize and adore personal deities.

Thus, in speaking of the theology of any religion, we have to consider also any philosophy which it may develop. For the conception of deity may be very simple and elementary, or it may embrace speculation on the origin and nature of the whole universe of experience. In theologies of the first type there may be practically nothing that can be called philosophy, either ethical or metaphysical; in the second type the philosophy may absorb the whole of man's religious thinking. There is room for a large number of gradations between the two extremes, and we may find the interesting phenomenon of a philosophy springing up alongside of a religion, and practically separating from it. Indeed the two may be antagonistic to one another, a position which most often occurs when a comparatively low form of religion is combined with a high degree of culture and a strong ethical sense. It is well worth remarking that progress in religion and progress in civilization are by no means bound up with one another, and it is possible for either to leave the other far behind.

The second of the heads under which we may group the phenomena of religions is the *relation between the worshipper and the object of worship*. This is central, and something might be said for calling it religion in a narrow sense. It is true that it must be affected by theology, for a man's relations with any person or thing outside himself are to a large extent based on the opinion he holds concerning that person or thing. But, alike in thought and in practice, the theology is meaningless unless it has this practical application. A mere theology may be interesting as a piece of speculation, but it does not become religion till it affects a man's attitude and conduct towards the object of his faith. It follows that there may be a very large number of variations in the kinds of religion, just as there are in types of theology, and that those of one extreme may seem to be diametrically opposed to those of another. If a man believes that the unseen beings who control his life and destiny are hostile, then his prevailing tone in religion will be one of fear. If, on the other hand, he regards the object of his worship as supremely loving, then his tone will be one of joy and confidence. If he holds to the existence of a number of divine or semi-divine beings who claim his attention, his religious practice will be very different from that of the man who has only a single deity to consider.

But within all these differences there may be seen a certain kind of similarity. Every religion—using the term in the narrow sense just indicated—involves two sides. There is, and must be, the attitude and activity of the object of worship towards the worshipper, and on the other hand there must be the attitude and activity of the worshipper towards the object. There is a divine approach to man and a human approach to God. The two interact, and cannot, perhaps, be absolutely distinguished in practice, but they must be distinguished in thought if the facts of each religion are to be appreciated.

(a) The divine approach to man is, for practical purposes, what we call *Revelation*. It may be made in many ways. Sometimes there is no actual appearance of the superhuman beings in visible form, but their presence is made known by their action in the material world. This is especially true where they are spirits controlling natural phenomena, or sending disease and other calamities. On the other hand, their activities are often beneficent, and many peoples believe that they owe success in hunting, agriculture, commerce, and other occupations to the favour of the objects of their worship. In some forms of religion men think of their deity or deities as appearing from time to time in human or animal guise, and, temporarily at any rate, being indistinguishable from those whose shape they have assumed. Other men ascribe to their gods separate and special forms of their own, in which they appear to men. Such actual but temporary appearances of the divine beings in visible forms are called *theophanies*. Often, especially as theology advances and the gods grow more important, instead of the god in person there comes a subordinate being, belonging to an order between the human and the divine—in a word, an *angel*. Here the divine message is conveyed directly to men, and the actual person who appears is simply a messenger. A few religions think of divine revelation in literature, and accept, as an authentic statement of religious and other truth, a book or collection of books. Thus, in several of the world's great religions, we have *sacred scripture*, though the degree of sanctity and authority attached to it varies a good deal as between different religions, and even within the same religion. Naturally, such a method of revelation is only possible to people on a comparatively high level of civilization, where reading and writing are familiar if not universal arts. Again, a human intermediary often appears, and two types may be distinguished. The first consists of *priests*, who stand

B

between God and man by profession, often by birth, and so have behind them a long tradition of their particular service. They are normally attached to some special shrine or other material emblem of the presence of the deity. In revelation their special task is to interpret signs by which it is believed that the divine message is conveyed to man. Thus the sacred lot could be cast and interpreted only by duly qualified professionals, and it is only the priest who can rightly expound omens, such as those derived from the flight of birds, the inspection of the entrails of a sacrificial victim, or the movements of some sacred object. The second type will consist of persons who, unlike the priests, receive their revelations involuntarily. To this class belong *prophets*, and though the same person may be both priest and prophet, yet the two functions are clearly distinguished. The office of the prophet is essentially personal, and does not properly depend on tradition or inheritance, though there are from time to time suggestions that these sources of knowledge are not wholly absent, and there is often a tendency to group action on the part of prophets. Moreover, this class of sacred persons is always distinguished by some peculiar and abnormal sign, which may affect his outward conduct or may be merely psychological. In an early stage of the development of medical science the phenomena of mental and nervous disease are often attributed to this cause, and the madman or epileptic is held to be a medium of revelation. In theory, at least, such revelation is always regarded as spontaneous; the abnormal behaviour and experience were those, not of the man himself, but of the divine being who had temporarily entered his body. Finally, there is in one or two religions a doctrine of *incarnation*. This resembles the more primitive theophany in one respect, namely, that the deity who wishes to appear to man reveals himself in human form; but incarnation goes very much farther, and gives a picture of a deity who clothes himself with human form and human personality for the whole of a human life. He does not simply assume a man's form for a short time and for a temporary purpose, but is born, lives, grows, feels, and dies like any other.

(b) For human methods of approach to the object of their worship we seem to have no one comprehensive term; perhaps *worship* is the nearest. They depend, naturally, to a large extent on the character ascribed to the deity. If he (or they) be hostile and implacable, worship is "apotropaic," i.e. it is employed to drive away the fearful thing by means which will terrify or overcome it. With nobler conceptions of deity other methods become possible, and there are two which are almost universal except in the lowest forms of religion. These are *prayer* and *sacrifice*. No doubt the former originates in an attempt to communicate with the deity as one man communicates with another. Normally, however, the subject or topic would be something which the worshipper desired to receive from the higher power. Mingled with this there would be ascriptions of praise, for a low conception of divine personality assumes a god to be as open to flattery as a man. With the development of higher ideas of God, men cease to think of Him merely as a donor of things which they need. Though they still ask for what they want, they aim more and more at a personal fellowship with the object of their worship. Finally, in religions where the divine is not conceived as personal, the place of prayer is taken by meditation.

Sacrifice is a feature of religion which is nearly universal, and, indeed, is conspicuously absent from the practice of only one "higher" religion. Yet its original meaning and purpose are still uncertain. There are two distinct elements traceable in it, and two wholly distinct kinds of sacrifice. One is the sacrifice of *communion*, in which a solemn meal is shared by both the deity and his worshippers. This may have its roots in primitive ideas which hardly rise to the level of religion at all, such, for instance, as "totemistic" views as to the relation between a tribe, its kindred animal, and its god. The other form of sacrifice is a *gift* to the deity, and is designed to secure or to retain his favour. There are forms of offering which seem to combine the two, a gift being offered to the god, a small portion reserved for his private use, and the remainder restored to the worshipper. This is a form of sacrifice which we should expect to find in the worship of a god who is regarded as the creator or giver of the particular material produce which is thus offered. As the idea of a physical divine frame weakens under the stress of advancing thought, it is realized that the deity cannot—or does not normally—eat and drink the offerings made to him in the same way as human beings do. His essence is not held to be purely spiritual, for the conception of pure non-material spirit is a very advanced idea, only possible where religion is tinged, or more than tinged, with philosophy. But his substance is more attenuated than man's, and it is only when the offerings made to him are similarly attenuated that he is capable of receiving them at all. So, while he cannot eat or drink (for these appear to be the grosser forms of appropriation), he can still smell, and the portion or gift has to be transformed into a savour if it is to reach him properly. This is best done by burning it, and though sacrifice made by fire is far from being the only method of presenting an offering, it is widely spread, and may be regarded as the most characteristic form. It is very rarely, however, that the whole of a sacrifice is thus "sublimated."

To the majority of us the sacrificial system of the Old Testament is more familiar and more easy to consult than any other. It may therefore be used by way of example, though it must always be remembered that there are few, if any, unique features in this system, and that it is selected for illustration partly because it is typical, and partly because it can so readily be consulted. All the features just mentioned are present. The sacrifice of communion appears under the name of the "peace-offering." A fairly detailed description of a typical ritual is to be found in 1 Sam. ii. 11-17—this is the "use" of Shiloh. Sacrifices wholly withdrawn from the worshipper are of two classes. The first of these includes the "sin-offering" and the "trespass-" or "guilt-offering." Of these the worshipper has no portion at all, while the priest receives the greater part of the flesh. In both these and the "peace-offering," however, the portions presented at the altar, as a direct gift to God, are strictly defined, and include always the blood and the internal fat. It should be added that the word which describes the sublimation by fire, the actual burning on the altar of God's portion, is usually rendered in the English versions "burn incense," though, as a matter of fact, "incense," as we understand the term, is by no means a necessary element in the offering, and is frequently absent. Those portions of an offering which are assigned to the priest (or, in certain cases, to the worshipper) are subject to a ritual in which the article is swung towards the altar and then withdrawn. This is the so-called "wave-offering," and implies that the gift is offered to the deity, and then returned for the use of man. The "burnt-offering" or "whole-burnt-offering" resembles the last class, except in the destination of the flesh of the victim, which in this type of sacrifice is completely burnt upon the altar. It will be observed that the terminology in English is apt to be misleading, though the Hebrew words and their context leave no doubt as to their meaning.

The priest also plays an important part in the approach to the deity. Gods are found by experience to be capricious in character and fastidious in taste. The frequent failure of men to secure what they seek by prayer and sacrifice seems to them to indicate that they have not understood the wishes of those whom they have addressed. Further, divine beings are often extremely dangerous, and men feel that they risk, not merely religious failure, but injury and even death, if the approach is improperly made. The belief that to see a god is to die is very widely spread, and the traditions of more than one religion contain stories of disaster following upon careless or ignorant treatment of a deity. The result is that men feel the need of a class of persons who shall be experts in religious matters. They must be persons who stand in some special relation to the supernatural, and are therefore able to deal safely with matters which would be dangerous and even fatal to the ordinary man. It is only natural that the persons chosen should be those who are recognized as being already in fairly close contact with the objects of worship. The priests are the guardians of the shrines, and through them, also, come certain forms of divine revelation. They, therefore, may be expected to know the gods, to under-stand their whims, and to regulate properly the human approach to them. Belonging, as they often do, to families or to classes especially trained, they have at their disposal the accumulated experience of past generations. This is handed down traditionally, and serves both to protect the ministrants themselves and to secure the greatest possible favour from the object of worship. Their functions will include the arrangement of the details of sacrifice and the actual performance of the more intimate parts of the ritual. That which an offerer does, he must do exactly as the priest prescribes, and there are some functions that he must leave entirely to the priest. The same principle holds good also in prayer, for tradition and experience have taught the priest the right formulæ and attitudes. Thus the priest has a unique position in most religions. To man he represents the god, to the god he represents man, and his place is therefore pivotal in many, though not in all, religious systems.

(c) It remains to note the purpose of worship, the aim of all that man feels and does in his dealings with the object of his worship. Here three elements may be clearly distinguished, though they follow naturally in order and may in some religions shade off one into another.

(i) In the first place every religion presents an ideal relationship between the worshipper and the object of worship. It is obvious that this ideal depends mainly on the theology, on the character that is assigned to the superman. If that which a man worships is merely terrible and dangerous, the ideal will be one of complete separation. The essential and characteristic tone of the religion will be one of fear, and all its practices will be "apotropaic." Men will want to keep their "god"—though often it is hardly accurate to use the word at all in religions of this kind—out of human life altogether. The presence of the spirits worshipped is manifested only in disaster, either to man or to his possessions. His highest religious hope, his deepest spiritual ambition, is to get these beings to go away from him and to keep away from him. It is interesting to notice how a belief of this kind frequently persists as an undercurrent in the religious thinking of people whose professed faith has reached a much more advanced stage of development, and how often a surreptitious "devil-worship" exists alongside of a genuine belief in far higher and nobler objects of worship. Witchcraft and superstition are still only too common throughout the world, even amongst people whose religion has, theoretically, no room for them.

At the other end of the scale we have the possibility that only a single object of worship is recognized, and that His character is interpreted as the perfect expression of all that is good in personality. In such a religion as this the ideal will be the exact opposite of that just noted. Instead of separation, men will aim at the closest possible association, and will set before themselves the aspiration and hope of a communion with Him which shall be perfect in its intimacy and unbroken to eternity.

As a matter of fact, however, in most religions the practical aim that men set before themselves is one of material prosperity. Gods are to their worshippers persons who can exercise some control, often complete control, over their fortunes. They may send game to the hunter, guide and protect the flocks of the shepherd, produce the crops of the farmer, or they may withhold any or all of these blessings. It is not only in the lowest forms of religion that the ill will of the superhuman is manifested in disaster; in the higher forms, however, the disaster is to be removed or remedied, not by expelling the object of worship but by securing a change in his attitude. He is credited with psychological qualities very much like those of men, and it is supposed that his infliction of suffering and his abstention from blessing are due to his anger, which may be removed if the right method is understood. In some religions the range of his anger and favour extends beyond death, and may endure to all eternity. We have thus a materialistic heaven and a materialistic hell, and the central object, the ultimate ideal which the religion sets before itself, is to attain the one and to escape the other.

All these are ideals which are natural to religions which acknowledge personal objects of worship. In that strongly metaphysical type to which allusion has already been made, where one entity alone is held to exist, the sense of personality is much weakened, and just as there is no personal god in the true sense of the term, so there is no personal ideal. On the contrary the best that such a religion has to offer is a loss of personal identity, and a reabsorption into the one ultimate essence from which the individual man has temporarily been isolated. But, different as the ideals of the various religions are, every one has an ideal. This it sets before men, and its whole purpose is to enable them to attain it.

(ii) In the second place every religion is faced with a

fact. Whatever the ideal be, high or low, perfect or imperfect, it is the universal experience of mankind that it is either temporary or unattainable. There is always something which prevents its achievement, and men always know that they have not permanently reached that at which they aimed. Further we have the practically universal admission, or even assumption, that the responsibility for this failure lies with the worshipper, not with the object of worship. The man who dreads disaster finds that it befalls him. The man who seeks above all things communion with a supreme and divine personality finds that this communion is hard to win, and when won seems only too easily lost. Both alike believe that the fault is with themselves. They say in effect, "We have left undone those things that we ought to have done, and we have done those things that we ought not to have done." This failure on the human side to fulfil the conditions necessary for the attainment and maintenance of the ideal is *sin*. It cannot be too strongly insisted that sin is not a merely theological conception, nor a fabrication of the philosophic mind; it is a fact of experience, and that experience is wellnigh universal. The explanation may be theological, but the fact is not.

Naturally conceptions of what constitutes sin differ as widely as conceptions of deity. There is no one act whose commission is sin in all religions; there is no one duty whose neglect is sin to every form of faith. It is not always easy to remember that there is no necessary connexion between sin and immorality. There is, as a matter of fact, hardly a vice or crime which has not been at one time or another, not merely permitted, but even enjoined by religion. For sin is a matter which lies solely between man and his god; except in so far as a man may be the representative of a god or is under the special protection of a god, no human being is really interested in sin beside the sinner. The character of sin, then, depends entirely on the character and demands of the god against whom it is sin, the god with whom it produces the wrong relations. If that god requires acts which violate the laws laid down by the worshipper's conscience, then the performance of these acts may be immoral, but it is not sin. Except in that very small group of religions which may be called ethical—small in number, though their professed adherents to-day are very numerous—sin is often concerned with ritual. It is the failure to observe some element in the duty which the man owes to the god, or the doing of something to which the god objects. The former may have no moral value at all, and the latter may be ethically unexceptionable, but that does not affect the question. It has already been remarked that gods are apt to be capricious and fastidious, and the sin may consist in the forgetting of some minor ceremonial detail. Except in the "ethical" religions man's conduct to his neighbour involves sin only when some divine being has expressly been imported into the case, and the sin then lies in the insult offered to that deity. The adherents of most religious systems would admit that it is morally wrong to tell lies; it does not become sin unless a god has expressly been introduced into the conversation or the bargain through an oath. Then falsehood is expected to bring punishment, but it is to avenge the personal honour of the god whose name has been profaned, not to vindicate an essential moral principle. There are, of course, in many religions gods whose function it is to safeguard certain human relations, but disregard or violation of the rules is sin, not because it wrongs a man but because it wrongs the god. There is, nevertheless, in all religions something which is recognized as sin, and it is that which interferes with the ideal.

(iii) The ideal and the fact together produce the problem—how man may attain the ideal in spite of the fact. Since the experience of sin is universal, a religion would be utterly meaningless if it did not face and in some way

attempt a solution. In so far as any religion left it unsolved, it would confess its failure to achieve its purpose,
and a religion which did not offer some means of over-
coming sin would at once cease to exist. In other words,
every religion must provide men with what we may call
*atonement*, though the actual term is more properly confined to some higher forms of faith, especially those in
which the ideal consists in friendly relations between the
worshipper and his god. But even in the lowest of religious
systems there is some means offered—though its efficacy
cannot always be guaranteed—whereby the offence that
human conduct has given may be wiped out and the ideal
relations restored. It is also clear that this must necessarily
be the actual centre of the religion. Whilst it may have
activities with another purpose, yet the problem that it
always has before it is that of recovering the proper
position, and eliminating the effects of failure. So familiar
and so universal is the fact of sin that in many minds
religion operates only when man is in trouble and
believes that his trouble is due to a breach in the ideal
relations between himself and that which he worships.

In most religions, then, the purpose of the majority of
the religious acts performed on the human side is an
atonement. It follows that there is seldom a specific type
of action which has this purpose and no other. Prayer
alone is often regarded as adequate, especially for minor
breaches of the religious law. Man asks for forgiveness,
requests that his god will overlook his fault, and receives
in some way the assurance that this has been done.
Sometimes it is necessary to prove penitence in more
drastic ways, and penance, sometimes self-inflicted in the
form of asceticism or even self-torture, is employed. But
the familiar and almost universal method of atonement is
sacrifice. There seem to be several ideas underlying the
various practices which have this purpose. Perhaps that
which is the most frequent is the belief that the favour of

the offended god can be bought, that offerings made to him will be of the nature of fines, which will serve to wipe out the offence and enable the offender to recover his old position. But certain elements in the ritual of some religions suggest that there is a peculiar, almost a magical efficacy in the blood of a victim which has been ceremonially slain for the purpose, for the ritual of atonement may include the application of the blood to the penitent and to the material representation of the god. Water is another medium which is often used, especially in purification from minor ritual offences which have rendered the worshipper ceremonially unclean. But some ritual act on the human side is necessary before atonement can be secured, a rule which holds good of all religions known except Christianity.

The third main head under which the phenomena presented by each religion may be grouped is that of *Ethics*. It has already been pointed out that in the strict sense there is no necessary connexion between religion and morality, and that in many religions the gods are interested in man's dealings with his neighbours only by accident. In many ways man's relation to his neighbour is affected indirectly by religion, for under some systems the whole social order has a religious sanction. But it does not follow that the relations thus produced by religion correspond to men's conception of what is morally right, and there are not more than five known religions in which it may be said that what is morally right or wrong is also necessarily religiously right or wrong. Too often the contrary is the case; religion and conscience urge men in opposite directions, and there have been notable instances in which men have deliberately abandoned religion in the interests of goodness and become atheists for righteousness' sake.

There are, however, cases in which a man's conduct towards his fellows is intimately bound up with religion.

Curiously enough, it is in the more primitive and in the more highly developed forms that this connexion is clearest. In "savage" communities life is a single complex entity, in which it is almost impossible to separate and delimit the areas with which we are familiar. A binding rule or custom may be social or legal or religious or all three at once. It is, however, also true that certain acts (e.g. "ritual murder"), which would normally be condemned in other circumstances, are not merely condoned but enjoined by "religion."

On the other hand, religions which recognize a single object of worship do, as a matter of fact, believe that their God is a moral being. It follows that those who would please Him or enjoy communion with Him have to model their conduct on His known commands and on the character ascribed to Him. The ethical implications of such religions may be so prominent that in some quarters they seem to dominate and even obscure other elements. We often hear such remarks as "Live and let live; that's the best religion"; strictly speaking this is not religion at all, it is ethics, though it may be an inevitable corollary of a religion. There is a real danger that a religion may suffer, not from being immoral, but from being too completely moral.

## II.—PROTO-RELIGION

IN trying to tell the story of the world of life, the biologist has actually before him forms so simple and elementary that he can regard them as primitive. The student of comparative religion has no such data. It is no longer possible for him to study objectively the earliest conceptions of the Unseen which entered the dawning human consciousness. We do not know, and we have no certain means whereby we may discover, the thoughts and feelings of "primitive man," or his attitude to the "supernatural." Geology and archæology may help us to reconstruct to some extent the externals of his life. We can feel some confidence in our guesses at his mode of living and, it may be, at his primitive art and culture. We know at what period of his development he began to use fire, and we know that, almost as far back as we can trace him as a biological species, he was interested in copying the forms which he saw in the world about him. He had a home of some kind—even the beasts have that—and from a very early period he became interested in adorning it with drawings of the creatures on which he lived, and even at times of his fellows. He early learnt, too, to construct vessels for his use, making them of clay or of stone. In some way he cared for his dead; archæologists assure us that human bones are not usually found mixed with those of the animals which are massed together in the rubbish heaps still found in ancient caves. But when we come to ask why he cared for his dead, when we inquire what thoughts, if any, he had about the spiritual world, we are forced back to pure guess-work. It is true that there are certain data which we can use, but they seldom give us clear and unmistakable guidance. Primitive man has left us the traces of his physical experiences; of his religious life we have no record whatever. Nevertheless, the attempt to reconstruct those elements in his life which ultimately developed into religion is most fascinating, and has occupied the attention of many minds, ancient and modern. We may say, in general, that there are three kinds of data on which students usually rely.

(i) In the first place we have the beliefs of the lowest and least developed people still in existence. These present us normally with a kind of belief to which the name 'Animism' has been given, a subject to which we must refer in the next chapter. But it is impossible for us to say that even the lowest of existing races or forms of society is in any sense primitive. Such communities as those of the Australian aborigines, the people of Tierra del Fuego, the Veddas of Ceylon, the Pygmies of Central Africa, or the Bushmen of the south exhibit a social order which has long since been transcended by other races, though they may represent a general stage through which many have passed, but it is clear that their social order is the result of a long and slow growth, and is often highly complicated. It is certainly very far from being 'primitive.' Hence we have no right to assume—indeed there are strong reasons why we should not assume[1]—that their religious beliefs, such as they are, can be called primitive, and it is practically certain that here, too, we must posit a yet earlier stage from which their present religions have developed.

(ii) In the second place we have certain survivals. (a) Some of these are material, and it is the province of the archæologist to make them known and to offer us an

---

[1] There is reason to believe, for instance, that the religion of the Australian native, so far from being 'primitive," represents a high stage of development.

explanation. We have such objects as the "barrows," round and long, and such customs as those of embalming, which seem to point to ideas connected with a continuance or a renewal of life after death. Other objects have come down to us from a remote antiquity which may have been used for a religious purpose, though it must be confessed that when we are really sure of this purpose the stage of religion represented is very far from being primitive. For example, examination of caves used by palæolithic man has sometimes revealed wall paintings which depict animals, apparently being killed by hunters. Spears are being thrown at them, or a spot of red colour suggesting blood may be placed over the region of the heart. Comparison with practices still current among some "savage" communities (e.g. in Australia) has suggested that these may be the remains of a primitive ritual intended to ensure success in hunting. A man draws a picture of what he wishes to happen, and so, as he believes, produces the desired result. But does the parallel offer us more than a reasonable probability? An immense gulf of time separates palæolithic man from the Australian aborigines, and it is not easy to be sure that there is genuine continuity of thought, feeling and practice between the two. Even if this be granted, can we properly speak of this as being "religion"? Should it not rather come under the head of what we call magic, i.e. an attempt to control the future by purely human action?

When we come to the remains left by neolithic man, we have to ask ourselves a different question: Is the type of thought with which we are faced in any sense "primitive"? Early pottery and, indeed, all that has come down to us from the later Stone Age, seems to be associated with a relatively high degree of art and culture, possibly also of social organization, and it follows that any religious ideas connected with these things may also have been the result of a long process of development. Moreover, we often have to guess at the meaning of symbols, and conjecture the precise use which was made of the things we have—and our guesses and conjectures may be utterly wide of the mark.

(b) It is possible that we are on safer ground when we are dealing with survivals in thought. In many extant forms of religion there are phenomena which remain as ritual or custom, whilst they have clearly lost their original significance. Certain actions are often assigned to reasons which impress us as the invention of a later age, which thus sought to account for facts whose true explanation had been lost. The use of blood in certain rites, for example, either lacks an explanation altogether, or demands a whole world of thought and feeling which has disappeared from the surface of the sophisticated mind. We are all familiar with the fact that countless legends and historical narratives are employed to explain rites and customs, though the latter may be demonstrably far older than the particular events to which the stories trace them back. We have several illustrations in the Old Testament itself, amongst them the explanation of the custom by which the priests of Dagon never step on the threshold of their temple, and the tracing of one at least of the women's wailing customs to the sacrifice of Jephthah's daughter. Facts of this kind are to be found everywhere in the history of religion, and some of the most highly developed forms include phenomena whose true explanation is only to be found when we can observe them playing a prominent part in a lower stage where they are still rightly understood and expounded.

(iii) The third line of approach is one which we may call that of psychology, or more particularly of genetic psychology. It seems reasonable to suppose that the race may well have passed through the same stages of belief as the individual, and that in the earlier days of each human life we may be able to detect feelings and attitudes which

C

were characteristic even of adults in the more primitive forms of racial development. Again, however, we have to admit a high degree of uncertainty. There may be some ground for asserting that "child races" think very much as children do, but it does not necessarily follow (though it may be highly probable) that "baby races" thought as babies do. And even if we were absolutely sure of our logic here, which of us would really dare to dogmatize as to what babies actually do think? We may observe their actions and recognize that there is intelligence at work, but we cannot be certain that our interpretation of sounds, acts, and looks is correct. Sometimes, of course, we can be reasonably confident. We generally know when a baby is suffering physical pain, though it sometimes demands expert knowledge—such as that of the mother—to decide whether the source of the trouble is hunger or a pin or sheer self-will. We may, further, well doubt whether such automatic reactions can be regarded as elementary or even germinal religion; perhaps the only fact on which we can lay stress is that smile it bestows on its mother. Is this the primary source of religion? It may be, but can we definitely assert that it is? In all honesty we ought to admit, in discussing the mind of a child before it learns to talk, that if there is any element which forms the basis of its later religious outlook, we have only the vaguest idea what that element is.

We thus have, in broad outline, various classes of data on which speculation must rely for determining the germ from which religion, as we know it, actually sprang. We must now notice three or four of the theories which have been based on the facts, and it is interesting to see how different are the explanations to which different students are led by the same phenomena. The following types of theory may be especially observed:

(1) It has been held that man's primitive religion was a pure and full ethical monotheism, from which he wilfully

and deliberately declined. The theory is clearly one which must depend in the main on the presence of such a belief in existing religions, and is chiefly held in connexion with a theological position appearing among Jews, Christians, and Moslems, though it has had some support in recent years from scientific students of comparative religion. But it seems, on the whole, inconsistent with what we know of the development of religion within the historic period. It is true that no great religion with a historic — founder has maintained its primitive purity and lofty conceptions of God and man, but this may be explained by two facts. In the first place, the founder of every such religion has been far above the average level of his time. A good deal of his teaching has been unintelligible to his contemporaries, and it has been left to later ages to interpret his words. From time to time there have been new movements within the religion, but as often as not they have been a return to the principles of the founder, or a new application of his doctrine to life. In the intervening periods there has always been a tendency for other elements to assert themselves, and the movement has been one of successive waves. In the second place (and this cannot be disassociated from the other point), the great religious leaders have always worked on the basis of an existing religious atmosphere, which has frequently been low. Men have accepted the new thought in part, but underlying their new belief there has been a foundation of the old doctrine. This has always tended to reassert itself, especially in the trough of the wave—the periods of comparative stagnation in the progress of the higher faith. This gives the impression of a decline, though the truth is that the great mass of the professors of the religion are only gradually shaking off old beliefs and approaching the heights reached by the founder of their faith. It is true that alongside of some of the lower forms of religion, such as those which we call Animism, we have a belief in a

single great god, but the history of religions, where it can
be traced, tends to suggest rather that this is a development from the earliest form of Animism, in the direction
of a "Polytheism," or belief in a number of gods and
goddesses. Mention will be made of this development in a
later chapter, and it is unnecessary to discuss it further here.

A similar remark may be made of the great Polytheisms.
Whilst they usually present the worshipper with one god
or goddess who is, in theory, supreme over the other
members of his or her class, it will generally be found that
this supremacy is due to the need for some sort of orderly
arrangement amongst the various deities. The analogy of
human society, with its regal or patriarchal figure, suggests that divine society also must recognize a single head.
The phenomena do not, as a matter of fact, suggest to
most scientific minds an original supreme deity; the whole
tendency (apart from the recrudescence of earlier Animistic ideas) is in the other direction.

(2) A second theory of the origin of religion is based on
the survival in many of the lower forms of religion of
beliefs which are generally grouped round the words
*mana* and *orenda*. The former word is derived from Polynesia, the latter from the language of the Iroquois Indians.
*Mana* implies a conception of universal power, which has
many uses and manifestations. It is as if there were some
universal electric current, which might be tapped at any
point and made available for the service (or disservice) of
man. Individuals may possess a greater or less share of it
themselves, and in proportion to their endowment of
*mana* they will be powerful and successful in such occupations as hunting or war. But other objects may also share
in it, and, when they do, they too have unusual capacities
and powers. It may to some extent be controlled by men;
they may acquire it for themselves or they may even be
able to infuse it into inanimate objects, which then become
to all intents and purposes personal. This may at first sight

appear to lend colour to the belief last mentioned, namely that religion springs from a primitive Monotheism. But *mana* seems to be in no sense personal, and can hardly be called an object of worship; it is rather a pervasive influence whose presence may lead to the worship of objects in which it dwells. This theory has the strong advantage of being based on a survival which can be interpreted without very much risk of error, and further offers an explanation of the rise of other forms of belief. It is easy to see how the distributed *mana* may readily assume a personal or semi-personal identity, and so may give rise to a belief in numberless spiritual beings, who may be nameless, but are nevertheless profoundly real to the human mind.

(3) A third theory emphasizes that fear of the unknown which, in greater or less degree, is felt by practically all of us, though it is far more obvious in the lower stages of human development. Lacking anything like an accurate knowledge of natural processes, man feels himself to be surrounded by personal or semi-personal forces which are beyond his comprehension or control. His mind is largely dominated by the sense of something weird about him, a something to which a distinguished modern scholar has applied the term *numinous*. It is too vague to be regarded as fully personal, but it is, so to speak, on the border line of personality. It produces a sense of profound awe, almost of terror, especially at night or in unfamiliar circumstances. From it evolves in due time the earliest form of "holiness," a quality in persons, things, places, or actions, which sets them apart from normal human life and imposes a *tabu*. Such a quality readily attaches itself to more clearly defined objects of worship, and it is hardly possible to doubt that in this sense of the numinous we may find one of the elements which contributed to the early religious consciousness and have survived in its later forms.

(4) A fourth theory is that which speaks of "pre-Animism" as "Animatism." This is properly the attribution of personality, similar to that of man, to inanimate objects. It draws not only on survivals but also on genetic psychology, for it is bound up with the realization of a person's own individuality and separateness from the world around. Until some degree of self-consciousness is reached, it is clearly impossible that there should be anything which we can call even germinal religion, and it may well be that man had to live for ages as a physical species before he recognized his own identity. It must be admitted at once that there probably always has been a "self-instinct," but mere instinct needs to be translated into conscious recognition before it can lead to a clear definition of personality. This is true not only of the self-instinct but also of the sex-instinct and the herd-instinct. Historically the greater number of the world's religions have had a sexual element, but though this may have had (and probably did have) its roots in the sex-instinct, it cannot have become a constituent element in religion till it had evoked conscious and deliberate reflection. So, too, down to a comparatively late stage (practically to the seventh century B.C.) the human unit in religion is less the individual than the community. Man never meets God by himself; he always meets Him as a member of a society of some kind, and true private worship is almost unknown. But whilst this may be a practical manifestation of the herd-instinct, it demands that the instinct should in some measure be recognized, and that a man should be definitely conscious of the community as a real entity to which he, as an individual, stands in a certain relation.

Self-recognition and self-definition, however, are slow processes. It is long before man fully realizes that within the boundary of his own skin there is a world which is apart from all the rest, and that he himself, with all his limbs (as long as they remain attached to his body), forms an entity standing over against and separated from the whole of the rest of the universe. It is even possible that men only realize after long experience that their limbs do form a part of them. A baby five or six months old wakes up early in the morning, happy and cheerful. It is just beginning to develop a backbone on which it can depend, and its first effort is to sit up. But it has not yet fully learnt the right distribution of its weight, and while the muscles bend the legs properly, it is not the upper but the lower portion of the body that rises. At once (let us admit that we are bordering on the realm of conjecture) it observes two moving objects waving in the air above its head. It clutches at them and eventually succeeds in grasping them. Then it plays with them, pulling and thrusting them about, till at last it applies the universal baby test and succeeds in getting them one after another into its mouth. All the time it does not seem to realize in the least that its own feet and toes are a part of its own bodily frame, or to suspect that they are more closely related to it than other moving objects external to itself.

There are one or two interesting philological details which seem to suggest that there is a stage in the history of the race when man is not fully convinced of the real continuity of his own body and limbs. One of the most obvious is to be found in our Bible. We are all familiar with the phrase, common enough in both parts of the Bible, but native to the Old Testament, "to put forth the hand." The Hebrew phrase which is thus rendered in our Old Testament means literally "to send the hand on an errand," and suggests a state of mind to which the hand formed a separate entity, with something like a personality of its own, though it is completely under the control of the owner. Sometimes, perhaps, instinctive or reflex action may lead the owner of the limb to doubt even the fact of control, so independently of his will do parts of his body seem at times to act. The action of certain drugs, particularly of alcohol, or some forms of disease, may lead to the same impression that the limbs have a will of their own, apart from that of the person to whose body they are attached.

It may well be this fact of control over his limbs which leads early man to a consciousness of his own separateness and individuality. They are far from being the only moving objects of his experience, but the others do not move in accordance with his will. He can use his own hands to produce movement in other objects; he can pick up a stick and make it strike his enemy, or he can throw a stone some considerable distance. But the stick and the stone move only in accordance with his will when he applies his permanent servants to them; otherwise they remain unaffected by his wishes. They are obviously not in the same category as his hands and feet, and they stand apart from him and away from him, and are as much amenable to the will of any other person as they are to his own. So he comes to recognize his own personality in the fact of his ability to control the movements of bodies which are closely and permanently attached to him.

Other objects, however, move, and it is only natural for a man to suppose that their motion is due to some cause like that which produces the movement of his own limbs or of objects with which they come into contact. He is passing under trees in a high wind, and suddenly a branch stoops and strikes him. He can produce similar effects, either with his own arms or with a stick held in his hand. The latter he knows to be the result of his own volition; is it not the simplest explanation to suppose that the tree itself is endowed with a will like his, and that it can move its limbs as he moves his? So personality is ascribed to it, and it is thought to be, like the man himself, an independent being, with the power of moving portions of its frame as it pleases. A man passes below a cliff, and a stone falls, narrowly missing him. He has produced effects of this

kind himself, and has thrown stones at his enemies,
human and animal, and at the creatures that he hunts for
food. What is more natural than for him to suppose that
the mountain of which the cliff forms a part has thrown
the stone at him, and thrown it with hostile intent? His
life is full of incidents which he does not himself control,
and his own knowledge of his powers naturally leads him
to believe that every object which moves—trees, stones,
rivers, clouds, the sun and moon and stars, to say nothing
of other animals—is really personal in just the same way
as he is personal. He recognizes in them the same qualities
and powers that he has discovered in himself, and the
conclusion is almost inevitable.

The strength of this hypothesis lies in two directions.
In the first place, it offers a type of belief, a theory of the
universe, from which Animism, the lowest form of religion,
could easily have sprung. In the second place, it corre-
sponds to a feeling which most of us recognize in ourselves.
It is quite true that sophisticated man does not really
believe, when he allows himself to think, that the collar-
stud, which has slipped from numbed fingers on a cold
morning and rolled under a piece of furniture, is endowed
with personality and a malicious will. He knows perfectly
well that the movements of the stud are due to forces
impressed upon it by his own fingers, by gravitation, by
the shape and elasticity of the stud itself, but at the same
time he is very likely to *feel* as if it were alive and auton-
omous. It is at least possible that we have here a survival
of a feeling which was also a belief in primitive man.

(5) In recent years attention has been called to certain
phenomena which seem to point the seeker after primitive
religion in another direction. It is noticed that as far back
as we can trace human thinking, even to those remote
periods with which only an archæologist can deal, there
are always signs of special treatment of the dead. The most
obvious and familiar of these is the practice of embalming,

best known to us from Egypt. It has recently been argued
that Egyptian thought was at a very early period dominant over the greater part of the inhabited earth, and its
influence has been traced across southern Asia to the
islands of the Pacific. It is also true that some tribes in
Equatorial Africa take measures to preserve the bodies of
their more distinguished dead, though the process can
hardly be described as embalming. All this suggests that
there is a belief, more or less strong, in a return of the
body to normal life. This is, of course, most clearly seen
in the elaborate arrangements made in the royal tombs of
Egypt, where the mummified king or noble is supplied
with exact replicas of the objects which he used during
life, or, perhaps, with the objects themselves. A modification of the same idea is suggested by a burial custom which
at one stage of development seems to have prevailed at
least from Mesopotamia to western Europe. In tombs of
a particular age the body is placed on its left side, with the
knees drawn up and the head bent between them. The
attitude is said (though the theory is contested) to suggest
the position of the fœtus in the womb, and it has been
thought to imply the idea that the grave is, as it were, a
mother, from which the dead person will some day emerge
into a new life.

Comparative anthropology supplies a number of facts
which seem to point in the same direction. Savage man—
we must now avoid the word "primitive"—notes that there
are certain marked differences between a living and a dead
body. From the former come breath, blood, saliva, and
other secretions; none of these is produced by the latter.
Hence it is supposed that these are not merely the products
of life, but the source of it, and they are recognized as
"Givers of Life." The effort is constantly made to preserve
the gift that they have bestowed, and round them has
sprung up a rich growth of ceremonial and belief. In all
ideas of this kind it is to be noted that the psychology is

of the simplest, recognizing only material elements in the human personality, and exhibiting no trace of a belief in the spiritual as contrasted with the physical. Additional support for this theory may be derived from philology, for in many languages which clearly mark the difference between body and soul, the word used to describe the latter originates in a root which means "breath." Such are the Latin "spiritus" and "anima," the Greek "psyche" and "pneuma," with their numerous derivatives in these and other languages. It is certainly clear that the contrast between a material and a non-material element in man is fully recognized only at a comparatively late stage of development.

The strength of this view is to be found in the explanation which it offers for many beliefs and practices found, not only in the lower stages of religion, but also in some of the more fully developed forms. It may be perfectly true that man has always—at least ever since he really became man—found it practically impossible to believe in the reality and the permanence of death. There are, of course, many forms of a belief in immortality, and the earliest known to us ought not, perhaps, to be included in the general study of ordinary religion. They are rather a religion to themselves, independent of that which concerns man in his ordinary life. The Greek Hades and the Hebrew She'ol (together with their analogues amongst other Semitic peoples) involve a kind of immortality, but they have no relation to the ordinary religion of the living world. The divine beings who watch over man during his life, and who form the proper objects of his worship, cease to have any control over him after death, and are even more completely cut off from contact with him than the human survivors, for the latter can, in certain circumstances, reach him through the infernal powers. Yet even Hades and She'ol imply a denial of mortality; the person lives on, though in a state very different from that of his former life.

There is, then, much to be said for the view that a desire for and a belief in a prolongation of existence after death is something that belongs by nature to man, and will be found in the earliest stage of his self-conscious development. It does not, however, follow that this was necessarily the source from which religion sprang. It may well have been a line of thinking which had a development collateral with religion as we normally understand the word. It is, of course, true that in all forms of religion as we know them there is some view or theory of the life after death, but it may well be that the two streams of thought remained distinct and separate till a comparatively late stage in the course of each. It is obvious that they did ultimately unite, and that in many religions each has very materially contributed to the other, but we may well ask for more evidence before we commit ourselves to the doctrine that religion is ultimately derived solely from a belief in the future life and from the attempt to secure it through one or other of the "Givers of Life."

It is difficult, if not impossible, to decide between the last four theories of the origin of religion, though the first of the five mentioned does not seem at present to be very probable. It is not unlikely that in the long run we shall be led to the conclusion that religion is to be traced back to a number of different sources. In its most highly developed forms it claims to deal with the whole of human personality and to cover the whole of human life. Just as any attempt to narrow it down to one side of man's nature or to restrict it to a limited sphere of his activity must in the last resort prove inadequate, so it is probable that no single explanation will suffice to tell the whole story of its birth. Even in the lowest forms known to us, there are apparently elements which are purely instinctive. Other features are the product of thought and meditation on the physical universe and its manifold phenomena. Others again seem to be connected with the feeling that man cannot really cease to exist, that even after that incident in his story which we call death there is still a continuance of his personality, though possibly under very different conditions from those which have prevailed before death. In connexion with this last point it may be noted that ideas about the life after death seem for a long time to form practically a religion by themselves, standing over against the faith and practice of normal life, and moving side by side with them. It is comparatively late in the history of religion—and then only in the great Monotheisms—that the same powers preside over and control man both in the Here and in the Hereafter. Alike in Indo-European and in Semitic religions, there is a great gulf fixed between the two; Zeus has no power in Hades, and in She'ol men are beyond the reach of Yahweh. Both in Egypt and in India, the deities with whom man will have to deal after death have but little to do with his daily life.

One more remark must be made. The truth of a religion is not affected by the fact that we can trace its growth and determine its origin. We do not explain it away when we explain it. The story of religion is a story of a great process of discovery, which in some ways recalls the record of physical science. The truth of the modern position in physics, chemistry, or biology is not invalidated by ability to go back to the earliest beginnings of physical study and speculation. The findings of the modern physicists are none the less reliable because we can show how they arose from the thinking of early Ionia, nor is astronomy discredited because we can find its roots in Babylonian or Sumerian astrology. So man's knowledge of God may have had the humblest origin, and may be traceable to the most elementary instinct and to the most primitive thought. But it does, nevertheless, progress, and its history is the record of a continuous discovery of God. It is, of course, true that in the process of development the explorer has often taken a path which leads only to a blank wall or a blind alley, and that from time to time old beliefs have to be entirely discarded. But no chemist to-day holds the theory of "phlogiston," and the validity of some of the old conclusions remains untouched by the fact that their discoverers were wrong in other points. Above all the student of religion receives the impression that he is watching the progress of the greatest of human enterprises. He feels that there may yet lie in front of him areas, oceans, continents of the knowledge of God which yet remain to be discovered and explored. Whether the fullness of that knowledge will ever come home to man none would wisely dare to say, for it may well be that a comprehension of the whole of the infinite may be for ever beyond the reach of the finite. But there is progress, there is movement, there is growth, and these things receive, perhaps, their most complete appreciation only when we realize from what lowly origins they have sprung.

# III.—ANIMISM

WE have now passed out of the realm of conjecture into that of fact. We have no longer to deal with hypothetical views concerning a primitive man who has long passed from the earth, leaving behind him only the scantiest evidence as to his thoughts and feelings; we have before us now the actual beliefs and practices of races still existing, and reliable records of the theories of people whose cultural development so far outstripped their religious evolution that they left behind them adequate data for the determination of their actual views. We have (i) evidence from the "uncivilized" races of Africa, Polynesia, and America—though we are beginning to realize that "civilized" and "uncivilized" are only comparative terms, (ii) the beliefs which underlie and accompany higher forms of religion amongst such highly cultured peoples as those of India and China, and (iii) a mass of literary material which has come down to us from the great civilizations of the ancient world—Rome, Greece, Babylonia, and Egypt.

Yet our difficulties are by no means at an end. Of the three classes of evidence mentioned, the first is rapidly disappearing, and even when discovered in time is often of doubtful interpretation. Accounts that are given to us by travellers of all kinds vary greatly in value, comparatively few being of the high scientific standard of the work of Canon Roscoe, Mr. Smith,[1] or Mr. Williamson.[2] Savage

[1] Cf. *The Ila-speaking Peoples of Northern Rhodesia.*
[2] Cf. *The Social and Political Systems of Central Polynesia.*

races are usually very shy, and hesitate to tell the secrets of their religion to strangers—for many years after the discovery of Australia it was believed that the aborigines had no religion at all—and their limited vocabulary and uncertain habits of thought make it difficult to be sure that an exact account (to say nothing of a correct explanation) of their practice has been offered even to the sympathetic, trusted, and scientific inquirer. The two latter classes of evidence are complicated by the fact that in both the living and the dead civilizations the earlier Animism is to some extent overlaid and modified by the presence of higher and more developed forms. It is true that these can usually be disentangled with patience and skill, but even so there remains the practical certainty that the Animistic theory and practice which have survived have been to some extent coloured by the later forms of belief which have been superimposed upon them.

A further difficulty meets us when we come to consider the beliefs and customs, not only of existing "savage" races, but also of more highly civilized peoples. No one can read such a book as *The Golden Bough* without feeling that there is a great deal of material which can hardly be classed as religious. A large number of the phenomena must be assigned to the categories either of Magic or of Sociology. The former is an attempt to control events by deliberate action on the part of man, and should probably be regarded as primitive science rather than as primitive religion. A particular event may be followed by another, and, with a very uncertain comprehension of the relation between the two, an unsophisticated mind may conclude that the second is the result of the first. There may, of course, be an explanation which introduces some supernatural being, but this is by no means necessary, and in some forms of Magic—e.g. in normal Sympathetic Magic— is entirely absent. Again, the social life of a tribe may be governed by an elaborate system of rules, many of which will relate to marriage and blood-revenge. Here again an Animistic explanation may be offered, but it does not follow that this gives the original meaning of the practice. On the whole, the safest method is to start with beliefs which appear to be concerned neither with Magic nor with the social organization, and to proceed from them to isolate the religious element in other practices.

Broadly speaking, then, Animism is the belief in a large number of spirits, any or all of which may interfere with human life. It differs both from the hypothetical Animatism mentioned in the last chapter and from the more developed theory which we call Polytheism. In contrast with the former it does not actually identify the material object with the spirit; it does not ascribe personality to the thing itself. It is practically never true that "the heathen in his blindness bows down to wood and stone" in the sense that he worships the actual object. In theory, at any rate, it is always a personal and spiritual being who inhabits, is represented by, or is in some other way connected with, the physical article that men worship. "Animatism" would make the stone or the tree actually a person; "Animism" regards it as the home of a person. Even though the spirit be most closely connected with the object, he (or she) is free to leave it at pleasure and to exist independently of it, in case of need taking up a new abode for himself. On the other hand, Animism differs from Polytheism in the fact that, strictly speaking, whilst the spirits with which it deals are personal, they have little or no individuality. They are "group" spirits, and though it may be true that only one of them is in action at a time, yet that one will have no name of its own, nor any other means of distinguishing it from others of its class. Some of the terms used for these spirits are interesting in that they have no singular, showing that they cannot be imagined except as somewhat vague and

D

indeterminate groups. At the same time it is doubtful
whether we know of any pure Animism in this sense, for
nearly always one spirit seems to stand out as personal
and in some fashion universal. This phenomenon may be
regarded as a first step from a pure Animism to a more
fully developed Polytheism, in which individual spirits
have become recognized as gods in the ordinary sense of
the term, and are endowed not merely with personality
but also with individuality.

As we have already seen, Animism is a term which
covers the religion of a fairly large proportion of the
human race to-day, especially in Africa, America, and
Polynesia. But there are Animists in India, particularly
amongst aboriginal tribes such as the Bhils and the
Santals—that whole group to which ethnologists give the
name "Kolarian." And, strangely enough, the popular
religion of China (apart from Buddhism) is an Animism
which, in essentials, is on much the same level of development as that of the African native. We are apt to feel so
thorough and so justifiable an admiration for the teaching
and character of Confucius himself that we forget that
Chinese religion as he knew it was simply a worship of
indeterminate spirits, with the exception of a single one,
that of the open sky, which had been personalized as
"Heaven." Further, it is still uncertain whether the term
translated "gods" in his writings means more than
"spirits." In these circumstances it is not surprising that
Confucius himself, for all practical purposes, left religion
on one side, content to recognize traditional duties and
perform conventional rites, while he devoted his main
thinking to the establishment of a really high order of
practical life.

To the list of important Animistic religions must be
added that of ancient Rome, as it appeared before the
contact with Greek Polytheism. This is perhaps the
clearest illustration we have of the whole type. As in

African religion and in pre-Buddhist China, there seems to have been one spirit who rose to the rank of a "high god," endowed with an individual personality and a separate name. This is the old Indo-European god of the open sky, Jupiter, and his presence suggests that all Indo-European religion was once on the same level as that of Rome, though the latter stagnated while elsewhere other nature spirits rose to be gods in the strict sense. But for the rest the old Roman had only group spirits without individuality. Some of these were spirits of the dead— Manes (a word without a singular) and Lemures. Others were concerned with the house and its duties, such as the Vestas (here we have only one to each household) and the Penates, or "cupboard spirits." These latter, again, have no singular, and are comparable to the "kitchen spirits" of modern China, represented by paper figures renewed on each New Year's Day and pasted up on the kitchen wall. Rome had also its outdoor spirits. Some of these belonged to the farm, such as Hercules, the spirit of the farmyard wall; Sterculus, the spirit who controlled the dung-heap; Innuus, the spirit who watched over the increase of the cattle; and Terminus, the spirit of the boundary. So we have also the hearth-fire which was the centre of home life, the Vesta. To quote a great historian: "Throughout the whole of nature" the Roman "adored the spiritual and the universal. To everything existing, to the man and to the tree, to the state and to the store-room, was assigned a spirit which came into being with it and perished along with it, the counterpart of the natural phenomenon in the spiritual domain; to the man the male Genius, to the woman the female Juno, to the boundary Terminus, to the forest Silvanus, to the circling year Vertumnus, and so on to every object after its kind. In occupations the very steps of the process were spiritualized. . . . The larger the sphere embraced in the abstraction, the higher rose the god and the reverence paid by

man. Thus Jupiter and Juno are the abstractions of
manhood and womanhood; Dea Dia or Ceres, the creative
power; Minerva, the power of memory; Dea Bona, or
among the Samnites Dea Cupra, the good deity."[1] But these
are not mere abstractions; they are felt to be real and effective persons who are known simply as species of which
single specimens may be localised or appropriated to separate human individuals. Each little homestead had its own
representative of every class, perhaps more than one representative, but they were individual deities. Latin has no
Article, so it is impossible to be absolutely certain, but
the probability is that the Roman (of the pre-Greek
period) would have spoken of "a Hercules," "a Terminus," and would not have used the Definite Article as
the Greeks did when speaking of their gods.

We may classify the types of spirit recognized in Animistic religions under three heads. These are (1) the spirits
of the air, (2) the spirits of the earth, and (3) the spirits of
the dead. Probably all are to be found in every Animism
known, though one class is sometimes more prominent
than others. Thus the outstanding feature of Chinese
religion (as distinct from the imported Buddhism and
from Confucian ethics) is Ancestor-worship. This is, of
course, a specialized form of the veneration of the spirits
of the dead. But Chinese religion recognizes also innumerable spirits of the air and earth. One type—the kitchen
spirit—has already been mentioned, but a very large part
is played in ordinary Chinese life by the belief in earth
spirits. These have to be considered when any new project
is undertaken, and not even a grave can be dug until the
spot in which the body is to be interred has been declared
"lucky"—that is to say, no spirit will be angered by the
disturbance of the ground. Until comparatively recent
years such enterprises as those of mining and railways
have been nearly impossible in China, owing to the fear

[1] Mommsen, *History of Rome*, E.T. 1894, Ch. II.

that the spirits of the earth would be disturbed and so bring disaster on innocent and guilty alike.

It is a familiar fact that the African native, even after he has received Islam or knows something of Christianity, feels himself to be in the midst of a world of unseen beings, who are always at hand and may easily become dangerous to him. Many tribes will hardly dare to go outside their huts at night, for there seems to be a general belief that spirits are far more active in the dark than in the light. It is impossible to enter in any kind of detail into the various beliefs and practices which result from African Animism; it is only possible to say here that it is greatly complicated with Magic, and that the "witch-doctor" has to serve both as magician and as spirit-priest. He has to know what methods will produce material results, what steps may be taken to destroy an enemy or to save a friend. He must also be able to prescribe the correct ritual when anything has revealed the efficient hostility of spirits, and to tell men how the spirits may be either coaxed off or driven away. And African Animism often has a specialized form which we must notice later.

It is less generally recognized that Animistic ideas which have survived from an earlier stage also play a large part in the background of the thinking of India. This does not mean simply that Hindu theology recognizes "Demons," who are degraded gods, the "Rakhshas" of Hindu mythology, but that in addition to the official religion (in which these "Demons" are included) there is a wide area of belief in spirits ("Bhuts"), which even education does not always dispel. A boys' school came *en masse* to their boarding-house superintendent one morning, terrified by the appearance of a "Bhut," which had stood for some time the night before with one foot on the roof of the school-house and the other on the top of a tall tree which grew some ten yards from the building. Nothing would persuade the boys that the "Bhut" was a figment of the

imagination. Such beings are thought to be particularly
dangerous to newly-born children, and a name such as
"Tinkori"[1] or "Panchkori"[2] is often given to an infant
in order to persuade the "Bhuts" that the child is valued
by its parents at only three or five cowries, and is therefore
not worth the trouble of seizing. The habit of placing the
hand before the mouth when yawning is often explained
as a protection against a "Bhut" who might be near at
hand and would enter the body through the open mouth,
so taking possession of it, unless he were prevented.

The spirits recognized by Animists differ widely in
character. Many of them are simply functional; they have
a definite part to play, a prescribed piece of work to
perform. Illustrations of this type may be found in the
spirits of the air who are responsible for the weather, the
rain and the sunshine, the storm and the fine days. More
noticeable are those which control the operations of
agriculture, the fertility spirits of the corn and other
produce of the ground. These may be regarded as normally
beneficent, though, unless they are kept in a happy frame
of mind, and assisted by sympathetic ritual to perform
their work, they may refuse or be unable to function, and
the crops will fail. The religious ideal, therefore, which
such a creed presents to its adherents is the harmonious
and sympathetic co-operation of the worshipper with that
which he worships. Sin, in a "friendly" Animism, is rather
difficult to determine. Some of the spirits may be angered
by the positive wrongdoing of men, but as a rule sin
consists in the omission of rites which the spirits in question are supposed to desire. It may even be felt that it is
impossible for them to do their work unless the right
impulse is given from the human side. The illustrations of
this type of worship which are most familiar to us come
from Palestine and Asia Minor. Amongst the pre-Israelite

[1] I.e. "three cowries."
[2] I.e. "five cowries."

inhabitants of Canaan we find that the principal, though not the only, objects of worship are fertility spirits, to whom the general name of "Ba'al" (=Lord or Husband) is given. They are rarely differentiated by individual names, though each place and district claims its own Ba'al, and probably does not confuse him with the Ba'al of any other place. This is one of the steps which lead from Animism to Polytheism, and forms a stage in religious evolution for which the name "Polydæmonism" is sometimes used.[1] The right relationship between the worshipper and the spirits is maintained by a series of festivals, occurring at the critical periods of the agricultural year. These are usually three in number: (1) the beginning of the round of the farmer's annual operations in the autumn, when all the crops have been gathered in and he is about to start preparing the ground for its new work; (2) the beginning of the corn harvest, which occurs in Palestine in the spring or early summer; (3) the end of the corn harvest, some seven weeks later than (2). Of these the first is the most important, and is observed with rites which are best represented by the Adonis Festival of northern Palestine and Asia Minor ("Adonis" is a Semitic word meaning "Lord," and is practically the equivalent of "Ba'al.") There are extant several accounts of this ritual, which in Macedonian and Roman times spread over the whole Mediterranean world, and the best description we have comes from Theocritus. Its central feature was the symbolic marriage and death of the god (for by this time it had passed beyond the stage of pure Animism), and there can be no doubt that it was observed in earlier times with rites which appeal to us as licentious

[1] It is instructive to notice that the Ba'al—amongst the earlier western Semites an unmistakably Animistic figure—has become a "high god"—Bel—in Mesopotamia and in Ugarit. The Phoenician Ba'al, too, whom Elijah and his successors opposed, was the national deity of Tyre and Sidon, and is not to be confused with the fertility spirits of agricultural Palestine.

in the extreme, though a more primitive mind considered them necessary to stimulate the fertilizing powers of the corn spirit.

It is clear that whilst in the main the worship of these fertility spirits, and of others whose normal function was to co-operate with man, was happy and even joyful, yet there was a certain capriciousness about the spirits which might lead them to refuse their help. And these were (and are) only a small proportion of the spirit world by which man is surrounded. Experience seemed to show that by far the greater number of spirits were definitely and deliberately malicious. For man to come into contact with them was dangerous, and their presence was manifested in accident, failure in the ordinary occupations of life, disease, and death. It is not surprising that the prevalent tone of Animism is fear, and that the religious ideal is that the worshipper shall be separated as completely as possible from the object of his worship. Almost any means may be adopted to achieve this end. Sometimes men attempt to bribe the spirits by gifts, and it has been held that this is the true origin of all sacrifice. Certainly sacrificial ritual often has this end in view, and is then described as "apotropaic." Other ceremonies are sometimes ascribed to the same sources; such, according to the very ancient narrative preserved in Exod. iv. 24–6, is the origin of circumcision. In other forms of ritual, too, we can see the apotropaic value ascribed to blood, and the early ritual of the Passover (which has numerous parallels amongst the less civilized races) illustrates a method by which dangerous supernatural beings may be kept away. Sometimes the ritual has the opposite aim; instead of coaxing the spirit into letting men alone, it is used to frighten him away. Thus amongst central African natives disease is generally ascribed to the action of malicious spirits, and the treatment consists in making all the noise that is possible in the immediate neighbourhood of the patient, in order that the spirit who has caused the sickness may be driven away. The fantastic and horrible costumes of "devil dancers" all the world over may be due less to a desire to imitate and propitiate the "devils" than to the hope that they will take fright and disappear.

It is practically inevitable that there should spring up a class of specialists in dealing with the world of spirits. They are dangerous and, at best, capricious, so it is only natural that the ordinary man, whose time is taken up with the regular occupations of life, should feel himself helpless when confronted with manifestations of the Unseen. He realizes that he needs an expert who thoroughly understands the nature and the demands of the spirits to stand between him and them, to ward them off when they approach, to expel them when they take possession of men, and to give instruction as to how they may be avoided. Hence arises the "witch-doctor," the "necromancer" (whose special business it is to deal with the spirits of the dead), the "rain-maker," and, ultimately, the "priest." He may combine other functions as well, and, in particular, may be also a magician, for, as we have already noted, it is sometimes very difficult to decide how much of the vague beliefs of a savage race are to be ascribed to religion and how much to magic, and the two are often confused. But, whatever his detailed functions may be, there is nearly always a human intermediary between the worshipper and the object of his worship.

The ethical element in Animism is very slight. It is true that Animists, like other men, make clear distinctions between right and wrong, and the example of pre-Buddhist China shows that an animistic religion is quite consistent with a very high moral standard and with really noble ideals of conduct. At the same time, this very illustration tends to prove that the ethic is by no means dependent on the religion. The two exist side by side, but they do not mix to an appreciable extent, and tend to remain independent of one another. Men treat their fellows properly, not because they will thereby please the spirits whom they worship and fear, but because they recognize and accept the claims of the moral imperative itself. In China, indeed, that feature of Animism which appears as Ancestor worship does seem to have the effect of inducing a very real and valuable reverence for parents, and tends greatly to strengthen and maintain the natural bonds of family affection. But in this respect China is almost unique, and elsewhere such moral influence as Animism exerts is to be sought mainly in the limits imposed on bloodshed (due largely to the unwritten but widely spread laws of blood-revenge) and sometimes to restraint of indiscriminate sexual relations. On the other hand, there seems to be no regulation anywhere of commercial life or of the social order, and whilst such vices as falsehood are recognized as morally wrong, they remain untouched by religion. Even in the two illustrations just mentioned religious sanctions are effective only within comparatively narrow limits, and the very principles which lead to restraint in some instances are responsible for excess in others. Murder, outside the narrow limits of kinship, passes without reproach; sexual license is often not merely permitted but actually enjoined; of a fundamental connection between religion and morality there seems to be not the slightest trace in any form of Animism known to us.

It remains to notice one or two religious phenomena which are or may be closely connected with Animism. Such a widely-spread conception as that of the *tabu* may have more than one origin. It is sometimes evidently a religious conception from the start, as in the Semitic *herem*, or "ban," which compelled the "banned thing"[1] to be withdrawn altogether from ordinary human use,

---

[1] The Hebrew word represented in the A.V. by "accursed thing" and in the R.V. by "devoted things."

and insisted that it should be destroyed if it was destructible. On the other hand, its manifestations in Polynesia are less clearly religious, and it may belong rather to the category of Magic than that of religion.

A form of belief known as *Totemism* may be animistic in origin. It ordinarily consists in the association of some natural object belonging to the animal or vegetable worlds with the human group. The creature is held to be the tribal ancestor, and is therefore treated with peculiar respect. The effects of this theory vary widely in practice. Sometimes, for instance, the totem animal is so sacred that it must never be killed, still less eaten, while amongst other peoples the most solemn religious function consists of a tribal meal of the flesh of the totem. The bearing of the theory on marriage is also important, and it sometimes insists that marriages shall take place within the totem itself ("endogamy") or, on the other hand, that marriage is impossible except with persons of another totem ("exogamy"). Intermediate between the two positions is that in which people may marry only members of certain totem clans, all others being definitely excluded. But the subject is far too wide to be dealt with in such a volume as this.

*Fetichism* is a specialized form of Animism, and is especially characteristic of African religion. The word is derived from a Portuguese term which means "something made," and this gives the clue to its peculiarities. Whilst ordinary Animism finds spiritual beings in all natural phenomena and in many other manifestations as well, the Fetich is an object in which a spirit is definitely induced to dwell. The "idols" so frequently seen in Europe, brought from Africa, are in no sense objects of worship until certain rites have been performed over them. The purpose of these rites is to place some personal power in the article, whatever it may be. It may be an artificially carved figure, or it may be simply any natural object; in any case, it has no religious significance until it has been deliberately personalized. Many of the carved figures with which most people are familiar have a cavity in them, and this plays an important part in the ritual, food and other substances being placed in it to induce the spirit to take up his dwelling in the object.

The effect produced on the Fetich by the rites of induction is not permanent, and they have to be repeated from time to time. It seems as if the personal power grew weaker, the spirit became less attached to his home, and after a while his influence, unless restored, becomes so faint as to be negligible and practically to disappear. And it should be noted that the presence of a Fetich, even at the height of its power, does not in the least affect the existence of the other spirits of the usual Animistic type. These are, so to speak, "wild" spirits, while that which has entered the Fetich is "tame" or "domesticated," and will serve as a protection to its owner (if treated properly) and as a danger to his enemies. Proper treatment does not mean merely the coaxing of the spirit by offerings and due ritual, but also corporal punishment if he fails to do his work properly, and the African native has often been known to beat his Fetich severely in order to induce him to confer the favour which his worshipper desires.

Under the head of Animism we may, perhaps, also include a form of belief known as *Polydæmonism*. Strictly speaking, this is a type of religion in which a pure Animism is beginning to develop into a Polytheism. Large groups of spirits are recognized, and each group is fairly homogeneous; all spirits of fountains are much alike, so are all spirits of fertility and all spirits of the mountains. But individuals amongst them tend to be confined to limited spheres of activity, with which they are closely connected. Some of these are local and some are tribal, the difference being to some extent (though not entirely) due to the scale of social order on which the worshippers live. The nomad clan will nearly always have some tribal spirit as its own peculiar guardian, though it recognizes the existence of innumerable other spirits, and may, at certain times or in certain circumstances, have dealings with them. Such a spirit very easily becomes a tribal god, and is nearly always supposed to be connected with the tribe by actual ties of blood. In other words he is thought to be the ancestor of the clan, whether he be a *totem* animal or a human progenitor. The important spirit to the settled agriculturist is the fertility spirit who makes his home in the spot where the community lives. He may have no separate name and may be exactly like other fertility spirits resident in other places, but the fact of his being localized means that he has an independent if not a marked individuality. The most prominent examples of Poly-dæmonism are to be found amongst the earlier Semitic races, and some allusion has already been made to them. The Semitic nomad recognized a type of spirit whom the Hebrew, at any rate, called "El," while the agricultural Canaanite and Mesopotamian Semite spoke of his fertility spirit as a "Ba'al". Thus we find each place in Palestine possessing its own "Ba'al," though as a rule these have no independent names of their own, but are simply known as the Ba'als of such and such places. The Dagon of the Philistines may have been also a fertility spirit of a type similar to the Ba'als, for there is reason to believe that the name Dagon is connected with a word meaning "corn." But whilst Polydæmonism presents us with features which resemble Polytheism rather than Animism, its main affinities are with the latter type of religion, and its ritual and theology alike compel us rather to assign it to this than to the next stage in religious evolution.

# IV.—POLYTHEISM

WE have already noted that all forms of Animism known to us in actual history or experience show signs of developing into something else. Alike in the existing types, such as those of Africa and China, and in the characteristic Animisms of the past, such as that of Rome, one individual deity stands out as a real and independent personality, yet with traits which suggest that he was once of the same kind as the other spirits known and cultivated or avoided. In all the religions noticed this one spirit has been that of the open sky, which has naturally a universality that makes the distinction between him and all others very easy. We noticed, too, that in that form of Animism to which the name Polydæmonism is given there is a strong tendency for one of the spirits to be adopted by a particular tribe or place, and so to develop a genuine independence. By some such methods we may assume that the transition gradually took place from Animism to Polytheism.[1]

Polytheism differs from Animism in that the objects of its worship are all independent and separate personalities, each with its own name and clear-cut character, each with its own ritual and method of worship, and each with its own separate temples and priests. As a rule some attempt is made to arrange these gods, and to trace family relationships between them, and this process results in

---

[1] The process has been sketched with great ability by G. A. Barton, in his *Study of Semitic Origins*, though perhaps he goes too far in tracing *all* Semitic deities back to a fertility spirit like Ishtar.

a *Pantheon*, or ordered community of gods and goddesses. There is also in all Polytheisms known to us a large mythology, a great body of stories relating the deeds of the various deities—not always creditable or respectable. These are sometimes traced back to the Animistic stage, and are held to be genuine "myths"—that is, narratives which personify natural phenomena, and describe their working in more or less poetical form as the activities and fortunes of beings very much like men. Attempts have even been made (as, for instance, by Miss Harrison) to show that the myth is really responsible for the religion, and there may be some ground for the theory.

In actual history Polytheisms have shown themselves to be unstable. The religions of the great ancient civilizations were of this class, and it includes those of Egypt, Babylonia, the ancient Teutonic peoples, and Greece—to mention only the more important. But the only conspicuous surviving Polytheism to-day is Hinduism, and even that shows such signs of modification that in its higher manifestations it is already passing out of this class into something like an eclectic philosophy. A superficial reading of the facts might suggest that the ancient Polytheisms have succumbed to the attacks of more vigorous religions such as Christianity and Islam. But this is only a partial explanation. No religion is ever overthrown by conflict from without until it has failed to meet the spiritual needs of its adherents. Judaism has suffered more from persecution than any other faith, and remains to-day one of the most striking of the world's religious phenomena. From the twelfth century onwards India has been exposed to the attacks of Moslem propaganda, in earlier times reinforced by martial conquest, but in the days when the conflict was at its height Hinduism still retained a very real and genuine vitality, and Hindus still outnumber Indian Moslems by three to one. Similarly Buddhism, though propagated by more peaceful methods, has failed to oust the native religions of China and Japan, but has quietly settled down alongside of them, so that a man may be (and most Chinese are) at one and the same time both Taoist and Buddhist. It may be argued with reason that in Europe and western Asia—to say nothing of northern Africa—the intolerance of Christianity and of Islam has been a powerful factor in the destruction of the earlier Animisms and Polytheisms, but it remains true that the converts must have found in the new religion when offered to them a superior satisfaction of their religious needs. That this is not merely the result of force is obvious from the enormous rapidity with which Islam has spread in northern Africa by peaceful methods during the last generation.

It would seem that Polytheism develops from Animism in one of two ways, which, however, are not mutually exclusive. Different spirits may be individualized, whether they be the spirits of natural phenomena or the spirits of the dead.[1] The process is perhaps most easy with the latter class, and there is a well-known theory called "Euhemerism" which assigns this origin to all gods and goddesses. But whilst it may be true of a certain number of deities in many religions, it can hardly hold good for all. In Vedic India, for example, the gods and goddesses seem to have been all deified natural phenomena, with a very thin disguise over their original character. Varuna is the god of the open sky; Indra is the upper air, especially as affected by weather; Ushas is the dawn. Few of the Homeric gods can have been deified men, though some doubt was thrown in ancient times on the divine origin of Zeus. But the rest are probably all to be traced back to natural phenomena of one kind or another, or else to some local or tribal spirit who has reached divine rank through

[1] There is some evidence for the view that Egyptian Polytheism developed (in part) from a form of Totemism, though this theory will not account for all the facts. Of all the ancient religions, that of Egypt seems to be the most complex.

the stage of Polydæmonism. The old Teutonic gods also are originally <u>powers of nature</u>, and the same remark applies to some of the gods of Egypt and of Mesopotamia. But in later developments, both in Greece and in India, the deification of human beings becomes easy and frequent. The earliest illustration in European religion seems to have been Heracles, who does not appear in the Homeric age, but by the beginning of the Christian era has become one of the best known and most widely worshipped of the gods of the Mediterranean world. Evidence of his popularity may be found in his identification with the Roman Hercules on the one hand and with the Indian Vishnu on the other. The deification of Roman Emperors, even during their lifetime, was a normal feature of the later decadent period of Mediterranean religion, whilst from an early period the royal house of Egypt claimed at least divine descent, and the fiction was maintained through successive dynasties. Even Darius I and Alexander found it politic to assume divine rank on taking possession of the country. In modern India, as is well known, divine honours are frequently paid to the spirit of a conspicuous personality, whether native or foreign, though as a matter of fact it will commonly be found that this happens more readily amongst people who are either professed Animists or have retained a very strong animistic element in their Hinduism.

The transition from natural phenomena to gods and goddesses in the full sense of the term is simple and obvious enough. But this in itself rarely suffices to form the ordinary Pantheon of a Polytheistic religion, and it seems that, especially amongst a people of growing culture and intelligence, other facts have to be considered. Many of the objects of worship attain their position through the stage of Polydæmonism. A god starts with a local or tribal significance, and then, either through peace or war, through trade or conquest, spreads his influence. This

E

method of growth can often be recognized by the fact that the mythology generally locates a god more properly in a particular spot, and assigns to him a peculiarly sacred temple there. The Mesopotamian Pantheon seems to have been the result of the political history of the country, for most of the gods are originally the deities of individual cities. Thus Asshur belongs to the north, perhaps not originally to Nineveh, but to some older place in the same district. Enlil—an old Sumerian deity taken over by the Babylonians—has his home at Nippur; Marduk is properly the god of Babylon, and Nabu of Borsippa. In Egypt we find that the conflict between Amon and Ra is also rivalry between Thebes and Memphis. Amongst the Greek deities Athene has her home in Attica, so too Demeter; whilst Artemis comes from the far north. Sometimes the supremacy of a god is due to the supremacy of his people; it seems to be for this reason that Marduk, god of Babylon, eventually attains to the principal position among the deities of Mesopotamia. Gods also migrate with their peoples; we have the record of the importation into northern Israel of a number of foreign deities with the settlers planted by Asshur-bani-pal. A commercial treaty might be accompanied by a religious fellowship. Traders would bring their gods with them and secure their worship in the land with which they desired to deal. An illustration is found in the story of the Egyptian prince Wen-Amon, who, in the eleventh century B.C., tried to establish a commercial treaty with Byblos, and (apparently) succeeded only in securing a recognition of his god Amon in that city. It seems probable that wherever the Assyrians conquered a country they insisted on the adoption by the people of some forms of Mesopotamian worship, and it is a significant fact that more than one attempt to purify the worship of Israel is associated with an effort at political independence and is followed by foreign invasion.

The adoption or imposition of a cult, however, was not

the only way in which the influence of a god or goddess might spread. There was often a distinct tendency to identify the deities of one people with those of another, especially if their character had something in common, or even if there were a resemblance in their names. In classical times all western Asia knew of a single great goddess, though she bore different names in different places. She is the Ishtar of Mesopotamia, the Astarte of Phœnicia, the Great Mother or the Bona Dea of Asia Minor, the Artemis of Ephesus, and is even identified with the Isis of Egypt. The identification of the first four (and one form of Aphrodite might have been added) is probably due to the fact that all were fertility goddesses, but the connection with Isis may be due to assonance. This last is certainly the reason for the identification of the Greek Heracles with the Latin Hercules, for otherwise the two have practically nothing in common. The Romans seem to have been anxious, on meeting with Greek culture, to show that they already possessed a great deal of what Hellenism had to offer, particularly in the sphere of religion, and nearly all the greater gods of Olympus were identified with spirits who were already familiar in Italy. Thus we have Jupiter=Zeus (a more justifiable connection than some others), Mars=Ares, Mercurius=Hermes, Saturn=Kronos, Neptune=Poseidon, Juno=Hera, Minerva=Athene, Diana=Artemis, Venus=Aphrodite. An interesting phenomenon occurs in the Mesopotamian Pantheon. The old creation story was originally taken over by Semitic conquerors from the earlier Sumerian people, and the name of the god who conquered the powers of Chaos and formed the world was changed more than once. The original god seems to have been the Sumerian Enlil, but the most familiar form of the story puts the Babylonian Marduk in his place. An Assyrian recension of the same legend substitutes Asshur, and there is reason for suspecting that there was current in Palestine a popular cosmogony of the same kind, where, however, the hero was none other than Yahweh, the God of Israel.

The comparative isolation of India has prevented Hinduism from receiving accretions of this kind from outside, for the invaders of the country, during the last millennium at any rate, have all been Monotheists, either Moslems or Christians, and their faith has admitted of no rival or associate deities. But the history of Hinduism clearly shows that the number of deities has grown very greatly since the Aryan peoples first pressed through the passes of the north-west. The great Vedic gods have almost disappeared from practical Hinduism, and their place in the popular mind has been taken by others. The official number of the deities of the Hindu Pantheon is given as 330,000,000, and, whilst it can hardly be claimed that this figure has ever been accurately checked, the actual number is certainly large. As has already been pointed out, some of the gods best known in India to-day were originally human figures, which have been deified, though the official theology reverses the process and speaks of a god becoming incarnate in them. To this class belong Krishna and Rama. Some may have a totemistic origin, though this is far from certain, and it seems more likely that such a god as Hanuman, the monkey god, or Ganesha, the elephant-headed, is a deity adopted from some pre-Aryan people and given a place in the orthodox Pantheon. It may be held to be certain that Kali and Durga (both forms of the same deity in origin) are demons of an earlier time who have been raised to the status of goddesses. They, especially Kali, are distinguished by a ferocity and a bloodthirstiness which seem alien to the true Hindu spirit. The tongue of the hideous figure which always represents Kali (Durga, on the other hand, is queenly and dignified in appearance) is kept wet with blood, and though in modern times the blood is that of the goat, there is reason to believe that in earlier days it was drawn from the veins of human victims. Like the Graeco-Roman religion in its decadence, modern Hinduism has shown itself extraordinarily hospitable to other cults, the only stipulations being that their adherents should accept the caste system, with the supremacy of the Brahmin, and should observe the sanctity of the cow, refraining from killing it and from eating its flesh.

Hinduism is, in fact, the most striking and in many ways the most typical Polytheism that we know. We can trace its history in its literature from early times, and it is usual to recognize three separate stages. The first of these is Vedism, which shows many close parallels with the religions of ancient Persia and of Greece. There follows Brahmanism, in which the old gods have given place to another group, and the stress is laid far more than in earlier times on ritual and philosophy. There is a temporary eclipse by Buddhism, with which in the end the old faith seems to have made some sort of terms, and possibly secured the expulsion of its rival by some kind of compromise. At all events it is only in the third, clearly-marked stage, to which the name Hinduism is properly confined, that we find the doctrine of the sanctity of life, unknown in Vedism or Brahmanism, and it is in this last period that the Hindu Pantheon has received its most numerous additions.

Modern Hindu theology recognizes a great trinity, or rather a triad, of gods, Brahma, Siva, and Vishnu. The first is a philosophical conception, which has little bearing on practical religion, and there are probably not a dozen temples to Brahma in all India. Siva has many forms, and with him are linked many gods and goddesses. Most of these are terrible and destructive, though a kindly aspect is worshipped under the name of Mahadeva (the great god) and perhaps others. To this side of Hinduism belongs also the very popular elephant-god, Ganesha, whom mythology relates to be the son of Siva and his wife

Parvati. Siva is especially the god of ascetics, though some types of devotee are, of course, associated with other deities. One interesting and important feature of Saivite theology is to be found in the theory that every male divinity is matched by a female. The male is the more passive and fundamental side of the god, while his "strength" or "activity" (*sakti*) is manifested in the female. In this way the two most popular goddesses of Hinduism are related to Siva, namely Durga and Kali. It is true that the actual mythology, especially of Kali, attributes to her another husband, but the philosophical explanation of her character is that she is an active manifestation of the destructive powers of Siva.

A still larger number of gods is associated with Vishnu, and these include some of the most popular deities of India. Rama, the great hero-god, and Krishna, the god of love, both belong to this group, and seem to have been deified historical figures. The relation between them and Vishnu is described as an Incarnation, the god "descending" (the word "Avatar"—Incarnation—literally means "descent") into the world and taking upon him the form and attributes of humanity. It will be necessary to mention this phenomenon again. The number of Avatars is theoretically unlimited, and it is easy for any new god to be introduced into the Pantheon in this way. In practice, however, Hindu theology commonly reckons ten, and with them all there is associated a more or less extensive mythology.

Whilst there is this difference in the grouping of the gods in the Hindu Pantheon, there seems to be no fundamental antagonism between the devotees of the two main classes. Many of the gods have different names, some of which are simply attributes or reflections of the mythology. Thus one of the names under which Krishna is worshipped is "Radhakanai," which means the "possessor of Radha," Radha, in the mythology of the Puranas, being

the favourite mistress of Krishna. Combinations of gods
are also not infrequent. Thus Siva and Vishnu are often
combined under the composite name "Hari-Hara," the
Preserver and the Destroyer, and this composite deity is
often invoked, especially in the ceremonies which accompany the disposal of the dead. And alongside of the gods
and goddesses of the official Pantheon (which is not as
systematically arranged as that of Babylon or Greece)
there are numbers of deities which must be regarded as
survivals from an Animistic stage, and were quite possibly
taken into the religion of the Aryans from their Dravidian
or Kolarian predecessors. The most familiar of these are
the sacred rivers, of which, of course, the Ganges stands
at the head.

In all forms of Polytheism, then, we find a plurality of
gods and goddesses. They have many different sources,
though most of them can easily be traced back to one or
other of the groups of functional spirits which characterize
Animism. Needless to say they differ very widely in
character, and it is impossible to say that the term "god"
has any moral connotation. But the gods and goddesses
are clearly-marked independent personal beings, and each
has its own place in an ordered society of divinities, its
own method of worship, and its own individuality. At the
same time the actual belief of most Polytheists is largely
tinged with Animistic ideas, and there seems to be no
instance in which earlier features have not to some extent
survived alongside of the more fully developed theology.

The religious ideal presented by Polytheistic systems
rises only occasionally above the level of material prosperity. What men seek from their gods is that their cattle
should be fruitful, that their crops should not fail, that
their enemies should not conquer them. With all their
beauty, the Babylonian "Penitential Psalms" show that
the conviction of sin to which they owe their birth is
produced by some natural or political calamity. The

Greek believed that Zeus might blast the impious with his thunderbolt, and sought to keep on good terms with a god so powerful. To this day the great Hindu festal period, known as the "Pujas" *par excellence*, comes at the end of the rainy season, when the crops are finally gathered in. The aim of practical religion is to secure the favour of deities who can powerfully affect the well-being of their worshippers.

At the same time there does occasionally appear a very different outlook and aim. The nobler minds, even under a Polytheistic system, feel the need of personal relationships even more than the necessity for material benefits. Friendship is the highest of all possible experiences, and men to whom religion means most recognize that the supreme friendship is that of God. They are not hindered by the multiplicity of the objects of worship which are round about them, but turn to a single one from amongst the number, and, whilst not denying the reality or the status of the rest, concentrate upon the one the whole of the treasure of their heart. This seems to have been the attitude of the famous Egyptian "heretic king," Akhen-aton, who found all his spiritual needs satisfied in the worship of Aton, and therefore sought to make him the supreme God. Whether his doctrine was a genuine Monotheism or not has been disputed, but at least it is clear that such an attitude must end in the recognition of a single God, and in the degradation of all His rivals to a lower plane. Perhaps more striking still is the genuine mysticism which meets us in some of the later forms of Greek religion (e.g. in some of the Neo-Platonists) and in some sides of Hinduism. The former may owe something to Judaism and Christianity, but the latter seems to have been a spontaneous growth, developing mainly on the Vaishnava side of Indian religion. For salvation, as conceived in some forms of Vaishnava theology, is not merely to be won through the recognized methods of

Knowledge and Works, but through Devotion, *bhakti*, the utter surrender of the worshipper's whole being to the god whom he loves. The noblest expression of this teaching is to be found in the Bhagavadgita, the "Lord's Song," a late section of the great Epic known as the Mahabharata. It also appears in much of the later Sanskrit literature, especially in the "Puranas" and the "Tantras," and it is one of the most terrible tragedies of human religion that from the lofty heights where it rose it has in some instances descended to the lowest depths, and presents its worshippers with forms of ritual which may be not merely immoral but even obscene and revolting.

We pass on to the direct relations between the gods and mankind. The commonest mode of revelation—one which is practically universal—is the simple Theophany. Gods and goddesses can reveal themselves to men in whatever guise they please, and it will be remembered how in the Homeric poems various divinities take upon themselves the forms of men, though they have their own proper shape, and may allow men to see them as they really are. But it is always dangerous to see a god, and the experience is usually fatal unless the god is especially favourable and has made the revelation deliberately. Thus in Greek mythology the sight of Artemis bathing brings about the death even of her favourite Actaeon, and the vision of Zeus in all his splendour blasts Semele to ashes. Even in the Old Testament we have echoes of this feeling: Manoah, the father of Samson, is astonished to find himself still alive when he realizes that the visitor who has interviewed him is divine. Similar instances might be adduced from almost every Polytheistic religion.

Essentially different from mere theophany is the doctrine of Incarnation, which is a characteristic feature of Vaishnava Hinduism. The theory is that the god can and does infuse a part or the whole of his essence into some chosen human being, and the man is himself the god. This

will occur at times of deep distress when nothing but
divine intervention will save man from calamity or point
him to salvation. Of the ten most commonly recognized
(though in some of the Puranas the number rises to as
many as twenty-eight) the first three are animal forms, the
Fish, the Tortoise, and the Boar. The fourth is a being
half man and half lion, and the fifth a dwarf. With the
sixth, Parasu-Rama, begins a series of fully human
Incarnations, continued in the seventh and eighth, Rama
and Krishna. Buddha is included as the ninth Incarnation,
and the tenth, Kalkin by name, is still to come, to end the
troubles of the present age—which is worse than any of its
predecessors—and to restore the age of primeval purity.
All Incarnations are not of the same quality. Krishna is
the only one in whom the full content of Vishnu dwells;
even into Rama he infuses only half his essence, and the
proportion in other Incarnations is lower still.

In yet another doctrine of revelation Hinduism stands
alone amongst Polytheistic systems. No other has a
Scripture, the revelation of God in literature. It is true
that Judaism, Christianity, and Islam all have a similar
doctrine, but all three are Monotheistic religions, and the
idea of an inspired literature is much more intelligible and
fits much more easily into the general system of the
religion. In Hinduism, Scripture is, curiously enough,
dissociated from the gods altogether; no god or goddess is
held to be in any way responsible for its production. It
belongs, indeed, much more to the philosophical side of
Hindu thought than to the strictly religious, and the
general effect has been to elevate Scripture to a level at
which it is practically deified. It is thus hardly correct to
use the term "inspiration" at all in speaking of the Hindu
sacred literature, for the word seems to imply the activity
of a single divine person.

There are two grades of Scripture recognized in Hinduism, and, theoretically at least, these differ in validity and

authority. The higher class is designated "Sruti" (=heard) and consists of literature eternally pre-existent and revealed to the ancient sages or Rishis. This includes three groups of books, (a) the Vedas or sacred poems, which are held to be the literary source of all Hindu theology and practice, (b) the Brahmanas, which contain directions for the use of the Vedic texts in the sacrificial services, (c) the Upanishads, which are philosophical treatises and form the source of all the philosophy of Hinduism. These again are divided into collections and books, and it should be noted that the two latter groups consist of collections which are technically attached to different portions of the Vedas. In spite of their very high sanctity, however, they (except the Upanishads) have comparatively little bearing on the life and thought of modern India.

The second class of Hindu sacred literature is known as "Smriti" (=remembered)—that is, books which were of human composition, though their "authors" did not write them, but handed them down orally. They were thus "remembered" by successive generations, though all are now known as written documents. These include manuals of grammar, ritual, and science, codes of law, both social and civil, and the later religious literature in the stricter sense of the word. The last class contains the great epics, the Ramayana and the Mahabharata, the Puranas, which are collections of stories about the gods, and the Tantras, mystical works of magic and devotion generally connected with the *sakti* side of Saivism. It is, as a matter of fact, these last two classes which exercise the greatest influence on modern Hindu religious life and thought as distinct from philosophy.

In many forms of Polytheism the gods approach man and make their will known to him by means of inspired persons. It is quite possible that here we have a relic of the old Animistic idea, that a spirit might enter, temporarily or permanently, into a human body and take possession of it, using it as an instrument alike for action and for revelation. The Prophet and the Seer both belong to this class, the former probably originating in Asia Minor or in Syria and spreading with the worship of their gods and goddesses over the Mediterranean world. The characteristic feature of the "prophet" is an ecstatic condition in which action becomes wild and uncontrolled, or, on the other hand, a state resembling catalepsy is found. The phenomena seem to have resembled in some instances the symptoms of epilepsy, though the actual manifestations varied widely. Descriptions of the typical "prophet" or "prophetess" are to be found in Virgil's account of the Sibyl of Cumae (*Aen.*, vi), in Aeschylus' presentation of Cassandra in the *Agamemnon*, probably in the *Bacchants* of Euripides, and certainly in the Isis priests of Apuleius. They are, in classical literature, confined to the service of certain deities, particularly Apollo, Bacchus, and the great Asiatic goddess—later identified with Isis. Another well-known narrative which introduces them is the story of the conflict between Elijah and the "prophets" of the Tyrian god on Mount Carmel. At times the ecstasy was artificially induced, either by drugs, such as alcohol, or by natural vapours rising from the ground, as with the oracles of Apollo at Delphi and Cumae.

The Seer is often confused with the "Prophet," and in common speech the two terms are practically interchangeable, probably owing to the fact that in Israel the two classes coalesced. Nevertheless the former is much the more widely spread of the two. As a psychological phenomenon the power of "second sight" is almost universally known and is often attributed to some form of divine possession. Even when it ceases to be attributed to divine agency, it remains as a recognized mode of foretelling the future. We may also notice the general tendency to assign all forms of insanity to supernatural agencies, and to regard the madman as one afflicted by a god, and therefore his protégé, and possibly his tool. The fact is that an explanation has to be found for any psychological abnormality, and the heritage of Animism may be seen in the tendency to assign to divine activity all phenomena, psychological as well as physical, which are outside the usual experience of men.

Other methods of the communication of the divine will may rather spring from magic, though it is equally possible that they may have a genuinely religious origin. Such are omens, whether derived from natural events, such as the flight and behaviour of birds, from the inspection of the entrails of sacrificial animals (especially characteristic of Mesopotamian and Etruscan religion), or from the manipulation of a sacred lot. All seem to be older in human thinking than any form of Polytheism, yet all are carried on and freely used under almost all Polytheistic systems. Hinduism is the principal example of a Polytheism in which they are not prominent.

The human approach to God generally takes the form either of prayer or of sacrifice. For the former to be efficacious it is usually necessary to have an intimate and exact knowledge of the character and whims of the divine beings. Hence the guidance, and sometimes the complete mediation, of the priest is essential, especially in the more developed Polytheistic religions. Certain formulæ are acceptable, and should be used if the divine favour is to be maintained or secured. It may also be that these must be associated with proper gestures and other actions. Some of the Babylonian prayer-formulæ show how careful the worshipper had to be to use the right names for the deities he was addressing. He might not know which god or goddess was responsible for the evils from which he sought deliverance, and he must therefore mention them all. Whilst at its highest prayer may be, and in many religious systems sometimes is, an attempt to enter into the closest possible relations with a personal deity, there is also the opposite tendency for it to degenerate into mere magic. As soon as it ceases to be an expression of communion and becomes an attempt to superimpose the human will on the divine, it begins to run this risk, and some of the prayers in Hinduism are (or were) thought to be infallible in their efficacy. Man could compel a god to grant his request; the god had no choice in the matter, and as soon as this stage is reached prayer has passed out of the realm of religion into that of magic.

Sacrifice is practically universal, and there is no Polytheistic religion known which can dispense with it. More than one origin is assigned to it, some scholars supposing that it started as a common meal in which god and worshippers shared, others believing that whilst this explanation may suffice for some forms of sacrifice, a more common motive is the hope that the divine favour will be secured by the offering of a gift. Possibly there is truth in both theories; many forms of animal sacrifice seem to have originated in a solemn meal, and, on the other hand, some of the objects now offered could never have been intended to be eaten either by gods or men. It is noteworthy that, alike in Semitic Polytheism and in early Greek religion, the flesh of the domestic animals of the tribe or place is never eaten except in sacrifice; in Homer, for instance, the "holocaust" (i.e. the sacrifice in which the victim is wholly consumed on the altar, or in some other way withdrawn from the use of the worshipper) is hardly known, and it is when men wish to enjoy a meal of beef or mutton that they offer sacrifice, giving a portion of the slain animal to a god. At the same time the presence of the gift idea in sacrifice is very widely spread, and probably accounts for most of the sacrifices actually offered in the historic Polytheisms. It should be added that there may well be other motives to be considered, especially in sacrifices which are used for purposes of atonement. Here it seems that there are sometimes traces of animistic or even pre-animistic ideas; the sacrificial blood is a living thing, indeed the very principle of life, and has an efficiency of its own in removing obstacles and in uniting those who have been sundered.

There seems to be practically no limit to the objects which may be and have been offered in sacrifice. They include animal and vegetable offerings, and every known Polytheism recognizes both classes. The extent to which human sacrifice was practised in early times is disputed, but in most religions there seem to be traces which indicate its former presence. It is even possible that a sacramental communion meal at which the flesh of a human victim was eaten was once common, though the phenomenon is only actually known in the religion of Mexico. But in most Polytheistic religions there are hints which point to an original human victim, for which, as men developed, they substituted animals of one kind or another. The animals offered in different religions and to different deities were, of course, limited, though taken all together they included practically all the domestic animals. Modern Hinduism, for instance, in spite of the theory of the sanctity of life, still permits the slaughter of millions of goats annually, especially in the worship of Durga and Kali, but other victims are rarely used. The ox, which in Vedic times was held to be a proper offering, is now strictly prohibited as a sacrifice, and, indeed, its slaughter and the eating of its flesh are regarded as the most deadly of all sins, save only the murder of a Brahmin. The early Aryans held the sacrifice of the horse to be the highest form of offering, though this does not seem to appear elsewhere as a regular victim. In modern Islam both the goat and the ox are freely offered— the latter to the great inconvenience of the Indian Government, for it obviously offers wide opportunities for conflict between Moslem and Hindu. Birds are often sacrificed, and even the pig, abhorrent to both Hindu and Moslem, was held to be acceptable to some of the deities of Greece.

The most obvious of vegetable offerings were cereals, which were either offered as they were gathered or else ground to flour and made up into cakes. In some forms of sacrifice an appropriate offering of this kind always accompanied the gift of animal food, and with it also came a libation of wine or some other liquid. Included in the vegetable offerings were various kinds of incense, and perhaps honey should be added. In modern Hinduism, where there is a strong feeling against the slaughter of animals (except in the cult of certain deities such as Kali and Durga), flowers are regularly presented, and in the worship of some gods they form the most usual offering. The nearest approach to animal sacrifice in these cults is the offering of butter, which is frequently consumed on the altar fire.

The usual, though not universal, method of presenting offerings is by fire. There are, of course, types of sacrifice in which fire is not used, such as the libation and the Hindu flower gifts. And in a few other forms of ritual the sacrifice is left exposed, to be eaten by beasts or birds sacred to the god to whom the offering is made. It is also customary for a part of the sacrifice to be handed over to the human proxies of the god, his priests, who act as his representatives. But, even so, some portion must be directly transmitted to him, for the normal belief is that the sacrifice is the food and drink of the god. But he is not of ordinary human substance, and though the idea of pure non-material spirit is comparatively rare and only enters in rather late philosophical speculation, a finer and more ethereal frame is attributed to the gods than that of men. Consequently as long as the offering retains the gross form in which it might minister to human need, it is unfit for the use of the gods, and needs to be "sublimated" or transformed into a medium which they can appreciate. This is done by the fire, which turns the material offering into smoke, and it is on the smell of this smoke that the

gods can live. So Babylonian mythology speaks of
gods crowding like flies to the smell of the burning offering,
and similar language is used of the Vedic gods as they
assemble to drink the fermented juice of the Soma plant.
It is the "soothing savour" of the sacrifice that the gods
need, and they receive it normally through the sublimation
by fire.

It is almost inevitable that in a Polytheistic system of
religion there will be many different conceptions of sin.
The deities have different characters and make different
demands on their worshippers. What one regards as
meritorious another views with abhorrence. Some are
satisfied with good actions within their own spheres,
others acquiesce in deeds which violate men's conscience,
and would not be permitted in secular life. Every virtue
and every vice may have its own appropriate god or
goddess, and as the number of these multiplies the moral
confusion increases. Yet it is generally true that the normal
conception of sin has little or nothing to do with ethical
standards. Unless a god is directly and expressly introduced, he is unlikely to take notice of man's wrongdoing
to his neighbour. Vice and crime only become sin when a
deity is expressly introduced into a transaction. This does
not mean that Polytheists are without moral sense or
necessarily themselves immoral. Millions of Hindus are
better ethically than their religion, and similar testimony
to the character of the ancient world is suggested by St.
Paul in Rom. ii. 14 f.[1] If, however, a god or goddess were
deliberately invoked, he or she would see that the crime
was committed only at the sinner's peril. An obvious
illustration may be drawn from the familiar custom of the
oath. Lying is generally recognized as morally wrong; in
a Polytheistic religion it only becomes sin, i.e. it only calls

[1] The whole passage, Rom. i. 18-32, forms a valuable description
of the moral standards of the ancient Polytheism of the Mediterranean world by an acute and honest, if hostile observer.

F

down divine vengeance, when the liar has expressly sworn by a god, and thereby introduced him into the transaction. Falsehood after an oath is then a personal slight or insult to the god invoked, and he will certainly see that the perjurer does not go unpunished.[1]

On the other hand, many actions which are not usually regarded as violations of the moral law are held to be sinful. At the head usually stands the omission or imperfect performance of ritual, and closely associated with this is the distinction between "clean" and "unclean." A person or thing is said to be "clean" when he or she or it is in a state in which it can enter into association of some kind with a deity. A stronger term for a similar, though more rigorous, idea is "holy." That which is "holy" is not merely fit for religious use, it is confined to religious use, set apart for the service of one or other of the gods. Any violation of a "holy" thing, any use of it for a secular purpose, in extreme instances even the touching of it by a layman, is sin of the most terrible kind. The idea of "holiness" may be an extension of the numinous through the *tabu* (see pp. 46 and 47). It is clear that in a non-moral religion a holy thing is not necessarily a good one, and it is also true that ceremonial and literal cleanness are not always the same thing. Another frequent type of sin lies in contact not with that which is too holy for ordinary man, but with that which is too unholy for any man. The contrast between the two may be exhibited in two regulations which are familiar to every one who has lived in India. The Hindu regards the eating of beef as one of the most terrible sins, because the ox is a holy animal; he regards the eating of pork with little less abhorrence for exactly the opposite reason.

[1] This is the real point of the protest raised by our Lord against the use of oaths; He implies that there is no need to take special measures to interest God in human actions. On the contrary, God cannot be prevented from concerning Himself with the way in which men treat one another.

It is not always easy to be sure what acts are regarded as sin in the dead Polytheisms, for so many of the Penitential Psalms which have come down to us speak of sin only in general terms. Men know that they have sinned, because calamity has fallen upon them, and therein they recognize the vengeance of an angered deity. But their language often shows (this is particularly true of the Babylonian Penitential Psalms) that they do not know which of the gods and goddesses they have offended; still less do they realize what particular act of theirs has brought punishment upon them. Occasionally, especially in votive inscriptions, we have the particular sin mentioned, and it is interesting to note how often it is a violation of some *tabu*, especially in sexual matters, though rarely a breach of a merely moral law. Fornication may be a vice and adultery a crime, but neither is a sin unless there are special circumstances which bring it within the purview of the law of some god or other, whilst in other circumstances either may even be a religious act, a "sacrament."

As in all religion, the supreme problem of every Polytheism is how to escape from the consequences of sin. In Hinduism, and perhaps elsewhere, the method of asceticism, austerity, and even self-torture is sometimes practised, but it is possible that at bottom this is to be connected rather with the philosophical than with the strictly religious side of Hinduism. If there is a religious basis, it probably lies in the hope that the offended deity will thereby be convinced of the reality of the sinner's penitence, or perhaps in the feeling that a man can escape divine punishment by first inflicting pain on himself.

But self-inflicted punishment of any kind is comparatively rare as a means of atonement. The ordinary methods are prayer and sacrifice, most frequently used together. It is unnecessary to elaborate the ideas and forms taken by prayer. On the whole they vary little as between the different religions, and in every kind of faith we find the same outpouring of the heart in penitence and longing for pardon. We have already mentioned sacrifice in its principal forms, and it only remains to note the special application of sacrifice to atonement. We have comparatively few data as to the ritual of atonement sacrifices in Polytheistic religions, and, indeed, the most complete account of such ceremonial we know is that which is contained in the Levitical Law of the Old Testament. Whilst these details are, in their present form, to be ascribed to a stage in religion which is no longer Polytheistic, but a pure Monotheism, there seems to be reason to suppose that many of the ceremonial details and the ideas which they express have been handed down from an earlier form of faith. It is quite clear that there are two distinct lines of thought which are represented in this ritual. One is obviously the payment of a fine, the handing over to the god of property which may induce him to lay aside his anger and renew his favour. This is naturally an aspect of sacrifice which is not confined to atonement rituals, but it plays its part here as elsewhere. There is, however, a more subtle and obscure feeling about the blood of the slain victim, which seems to have a peculiar power and unique place in the ritual. It has a double destination, the greater part being dashed against the base of the altar and a little applied to the "horns" of the altar of incense. This may well be a peculiarity of the Jewish ritual, for there is little evidence to show that other religions (Babylon is a possible exception) employed two altars in the sanctuary. But it may well be that the ritual application of the blood to the altar expresses a feeling which is much wider than Israel. Blood is life, and the application of the blood is a symbol of the consecration of the life of the victim, and possibly also of the worshipper, to the deity. It may well be that the thought which underlies a great deal of sacrificial ritual is the sense that by his sin the worshipper has forfeited his life, and he brings the animal which is to be slain, not merely as a present to his god, but also as a surrogate for himself. As he lays his hands on its head he transfers to it all his responsibilities and guilt, and it suffers in his stead that punishment which would otherwise have been his due. It is very difficult, not only in dealing with Judaism, but in thinking of other religions as well, to get rid of the thought that one element in the theory of sacrifice is that of substitution.

# V.—PHILOSOPHY AND RELIGION

IT has already been remarked that there are always visible in a Polytheistic religion tendencies which make for decay and, ultimately, for extinction. From a comparatively simple and noble nature worship, or an association of local and tribal deities, it expands by the inclusion of other elements, many of them of lower type than the original faith, and all of them making for complication, and in the end for confusion. There seems to be in the mind of the average man a genuine religious longing for personal relationships of some kind with the unseen world, and this a Polytheism satisfies to the full, for the worshipper can make his choice from amongst the numerous deities presented to him, and, if he so desire, devote himself to one alone. Such a type of religion is called Monolatry, and whilst it does not deny the existence of other gods and goddesses, or attempt to minimize their validity and authority for other people, it does exclude them from the religious life of the devotee himself. Not infrequently we have instances of whole nations or tribes maintaining a monolatrous worship in the midst of other peoples, neither developing into a Polytheism on the one hand nor into a Monotheism on the other. Such a form of religion seems to have been the ideal of the nobler elements in Israel in pre-exilic days.

A Monolatry, then, either personal, tribal, or national, may satisfy the demands of the religious spirit on one side. But there is also in the man's spirit something which insists on asking questions about the world and about human and divine relations with it. There is a search for unity, for a single principle or "law" which will provide an explanation for all that man sees about him. This philosophical instinct varies a great deal in different people and in different races, but in greater or less degree it is nearly always present. The Indo-European mind, perhaps more than any other, finds itself impelled on this quest for an Ultimate, and it is a striking fact that both the great civilized and developed Polytheisms of the Indo-European peoples—the religions of Greece and India—need to be studied alongside of the philosophy which accompanies them.

There is yet another impulse which must be taken into account. That is the demand for morality. It is impossible here to discuss the origin, nature, authority, and validity of conscience, but the fact must be admitted that everywhere men do seem to recognize the difference between moral right and wrong. It may be true that there is the widest possible variation in the list of acts and thoughts which different people would regard as right or wrong, but that does not alter the fact that there is such a thing as a moral sense, and that its absence argues some kind of spiritual deformity. As we have already seen, no Polytheism gives to this moral sense the satisfaction that it needs. Men have to go their own way, and work out their own ethical problems, and when these are solved it does not always follow that the solution is a religious one, or that it can ever be held concurrently with the ordinary religious belief. As a matter of fact, in the Graeco-Roman world metaphysical and moral philosophy broke away from religion altogether until the two found some common home in Neo-Platonism, whilst in India there is a professed alliance between the two, so that whilst it may not be difficult to assign some ideas to a religious origin and others to philosophy, the average Hindu is probably entirely unconscious of any difference between the two.

The earliest Greek philosophy is found in Ionia, where a succession of thinkers tried to discover a universal essence to which all phenomena might be reduced. Four elements, earth, air, fire, and water, were recognized, and one or other of these, or a combination of two or more, was held to be the primeval entity from which all else was sprung. Gradually the distinction between mind and matter was realized. The main centre of thought was transferred from Asiatic to European Greece, and the greatest of all philosophers, Plato, was an Athenian. His system and theory form, in fact, the centre of all Greek metaphysical thinking. His main doctrine is the familiar theory of Ideas. All phenomena and all abstract qualities, to Plato's mind, were copies or imitations of a perfect and spiritual "idea." In proportion as they approximate to that idea, they attain perfection themselves, but absolute perfection would not be claimed for anything within the ordinary range of human experience. It follows that phenomena can only exist when the ideas of them exist already, and the former will be, in fact, dependent on the latter. The ideas must, however, have a common centre, home, and origin, and this Plato finds in an eternal and supreme "mind." His explanation of the Universe, then, is that it depends on, and, indeed, exists in, an ultimate spiritual reality which gives it birth and maintains it. Whilst not directly Pantheistic in the full sense of the term, Plato's doctrines contain within them the germ of a Pantheistic view of the Universe, which manifested itself unmistakably in later Greek thinkers, notably in the Stoics and the Neo-Platonists.

The relation in Plato's own mind between philosophy and religion is far from clear. There is no direct repudiation of the common faiths of his day, and the last words he attributes to Socrates are a direct admission of a religious duty. At times also we find language which suggests the piety of a devout mind, and it seems that he never faced the difficulty of reconciling his metaphysics with an ordinary belief in the gods and goddesses of Greece. This may in part be due to the fact that he does not seem to have felt keenly the contradiction between religion and ethics, and, compared with the level he attained in the realm of pure thought, his moral demands, though high, were not conspicuously so. He held strongly to a belief in the immortality of the soul, like many thinking Greeks, regarding man as a soul temporarily imprisoned in a material body. The death of the body, however, did not mean final liberation from the chains of the physical, for man might be or would be reincarnate in some other earthly shape. This doctrine, known as "transmigration" or "metempsychosis," was not original with him, having been taught by others long before his time, notably by Pythagoras, and we shall meet it again in other peoples. But it is important to notice that it was a psychological and philosophical doctrine rather than a religious conviction. It was due to the nature of man that he was immortal, and his immortality had little bearing on his religion. Presumably in another life he would stand on the same footing as regards the gods as he did in his present life, and though Plato attributes to Socrates the hope that after death he would enjoy the company of the gods and of the heroes of old time, he himself elsewhere does not seem to have made much use of the thought.

Other thinkers of the ancient world—not necessarily philosophers—were revolted by the moral weaknesses of popular religion. Most conspicuous amongst these were Euripides and Lucretius, who earned for themselves the reputation of Atheism. In a certain sense the charge was justified. Euripides was a man with a burning passion for truth and purity, and much of his best work consists in merciless satire on the shams and follies of life and religion. To him nothing was sacred unless it had some noble quality of its own that sanctified it. He challenged accepted beliefs to justify themselves, and usually found them wanting. His *Medea* is the most ruthless exposure of the hypocrisy of civilization that has ever been penned, and a fair proportion of his extant plays would bear as a subtitle *The Hero Unmasked*. The gods as popularly conceived were not free from his criticism, and one of the most terrible plays that we know is his *Ion*. His purpose seems to have been to depict the great, noble, popular god of light, Apollo, as a consummate blackguard, cowardly, sensuous, and callous. Like most of his plays, this finishes, it is true, with some kind of reconciliation or reversal of fortune, but this is very obviously a concession to the popular taste, which always prefers to have a happy ending.

Lucretius is more directly outspoken than even Euripides. An Epicurean by conviction, he represents the noblest side of that strange philosophy, and shows his readers the mind of a great poet in whom ethical considerations dwarfed everything else. He had, of course, no belief in immortality, and the pure moral instinct formed his only guide in life. It is a little strange to find that his great poem opens with an invocation of Venus, but the passage stands alone. There can be no doubt about the whole-hearted fashion in which he discards contemporary religion, for at the outset he faces and meets the charge that his philosophical and scientific investigations will lead men into wickedness and impiety. His answer is a bold challenge to religion itself, conveyed in a word-picture of the sacrifice of Iphigenia, comparable for dignity and power only with Æschylus' description of the same scene. The passage closes with one of the bitterest lines ever written:

*"Tantum religio potuit suadere malorum."*
*"Such are the iniquities to which religion can impel men."*

Lucretius was a man who definitely and deliberately discarded religion because he found it incompatible with righteousness.

As we have already noted, Indian philosophy differs from that of Greece in this striking particular: it never divorced itself formally from practical religion. The Upanishads, which are the literary source for the orthodox philosophy (known as the Vedanta, the end of the Veda, that to which the Veda leads), are included in the more sacred group of Hindu writings known as the Sruti. Their language is at first somewhat obscure to the foreigner, even in translation, and though the main tenets are clear, there is room for disagreement as to details. It is not every student of the Upanishads who would assent to the use made of them by Jung, who finds in them a clearly expressed contrast between the "extroverted" and the "introverted" temperaments. There is, however, no doubt that in the quest of the Ultimate, the Indian thinker has gone farther than any other, and has developed a pure Pantheism. His essential doctrine is expressed in the Sanskrit formula *Ekam eba advitvyam*—"ONE exists without a second." That is to say the Universe, including the material and the spiritual, the human and the divine, forms only a single entity. It is eternal and strictly without predicate; some would even say that we cannot posit either its existence or its non-existence. The appearance of distinct phenomena and the impression of independent personality are either temporary or illusory. There is one very famous passage in the Chhandogya Upanishad in which a father instructs his son. He tells him to perform certain acts, to split, for instance, a seed till he reaches its very centre, or to dissolve salt in water. In each operation the boy reaches a point at which he finds nothing at all. There is a void in the centre of the seed, and the salt no longer appears in the water. Yet that invisible thing—or should it be nothing?—is the ultimate essence, and is to be identified, not only with the phenomenal universe, but with the boy himself: "That which is the subtile essence, in it all that exists has its self. It is the True. It is the Self, and thou, O Svetaketu, art it."

The problem of the origin of phenomena is approached and solved in various ways. The best-known answer to the question "How does the universe as we know it spring from this Ultimate?" is found in the Upanishad just quoted. The Ultimate (the Sat, literally the True) by thought evolved fire. From fire was produced water, and from water earth. Then the Sat, entering into these three elements, ·gave rise to various forms, shapes, and colours. None of them, as we see them, is pure; earthly fire has in it the elements of water and of earth, and so the others are in a certain sense mixed, though the mixture is not so complicated as it is in such organisms as the human body.

With this is bound up the doctrine of transmigration. In the form with which we meet in the Upanishads, this is not strictly a religious dogma, for it has no relation to the gods whom the Hindu worships. In sleep a man returns for the time being to the ultimate from which he has temporarily emerged, and comes back to his own body when he awakes. So when he dies he is for the time re-absorbed in the universal essence, but when he returns to a corporeal frame the old one is no longer there to receive him, and he finds a home in some other. The later Hindu-ism adopted this teaching and wove it into the religious system. The gods, like men, are part of the Sat, and in the end must return to it. But there are various births through which they, as well as men, must pass, though they main-tain their position throughout the whole of the present age. In the meantime they dwell each in his own appro-priate heaven (or, in the case of the lower gods or demons —the "Asuras"—in his appropriate hell) and men may find their new birth, not only on earth, but in one of the heavens or hells. Here an ethical element is introduced, for the next and some subsequent births are determined by a man's behaviour in the present. If his life has been normally but not markedly good, he will reappear on earth; if especially bad, then his next birth will be in one of the hells; if particularly good, then in one of the heavens. There is thus some sanction for the moral law in practical Hinduism, though the absence of memory, that link which alone secures continuity of personality, tends to weaken the ethical influence of the doctrine. Men are not greatly attracted to virtue (though there is in the best men *some* attraction) by the belief that in time to come a person who is only formally identified with them will profit by their good behaviour. On the other hand the ordinary doctrine of transmigration, as understood by the average Hindu, involves a fatalism which is a distinct hindrance to moral development. For the principle works not only forwards but backwards, and, however much a man may seem to be a free agent, his thoughts, words, and actions are in reality controlled by the life of another whom he does not remember, and in whom he has no interest.

It is impossible to leave the subject of Hinduism without a passing reference to the institution known as *caste*. Nothing illustrates more strikingly the extraordinary medley of thought and custom which modern Hinduism presents to the student. As far as can be ascertained it is neither religious nor philosophical in origin, and yet it plays a larger part in Hindu life than any other doctrine or practice. It may be that it arose in various distinctions between different functions in the community, for the four original castes of the Rig-Veda and the Laws of Manu were occupational, and there are still trades which are confined to members of particular castes. On the other hand it may be due to successive waves of Aryan invasion, each of which mingled its blood less completely than its predecessors with that of the aboriginal and Dravidian peoples. Distinctions of the same kind appear in the social order of other nations and races. Ancient Babylon had three orders of freemen, the noble, the gentleman, and the commoner. The Anglo-Saxon communities recognized differences between Eorl and Ceorl, and early Rome was divided into Patrician and Plebeian. But whereas in all other peoples the tendency has been to break down distinctions and reduce differences, in India they have grown and strengthened, till to-day there are innumerable castes up and down the country, and the rules are so many and so rigid as to govern practically the whole life of the people. Further, whilst elsewhere the "castes" may have kept themselves apart in blood and enjoyed different privileges, yet there seems to be no evidence to show that anywhere else the separation has been carried to such extreme lengths. No doubt there are and always have been ceremonial regulations affecting the purity of food, but it would be hard to find a parallel to the case of a man who deliberately chose death rather than take medicine which he believed to have been prepared by a person of caste inferior to his own.

The main facts of caste are familiar to everyone. It is partly, but only partly, social organization. A man is born into a caste—that of his parents—and if he comes of a family which is outside the regular caste system, such as the "Pariahs" of southern India or the Nama-Sudras of Bengal, there is absolutely no means whereby he can enter one. He must marry within the caste into which he is born, and he must enter one of a limited number of trades and professions which are open to his caste. In particular he must never take food which has been prepared or even touched after preparation by a person of inferior caste, nor must he eat in the presence of persons of any other caste, lower or higher. The very touch of some castes is pollution to their superiors, and the lowest of all are not allowed to come within a certain distance of men of higher rank. Whilst it would not be true to say that each caste has its own god and its own cultus, there are

forms of worship which are confined to one or to a few
castes.

All this is more social than religious, yet modern
Hinduism depends more on caste than on anything else
for its preservation, and caste rules are enforced by
sanctions far more terrible to the average Hindu than
those offered by religion. There is no one word in common
use which will always translate the English "caste"; if
the stress is laid on descent, a word meaning "race" or
"birth" (*jat*) will be used, but if it be a question of the
duties and limitations imposed by caste the word usually
rendered "religion" (*dharma*) is employed. The term for
"atonement" (*prayaschitta*) is commonly employed, not
only to describe the restoration of an offender to divine
favour, but to indicate the ceremonies by which a person
who has infringed some caste regulation may be reinstated.

The extreme penalty for the infringement of caste
regulations is exclusion from the caste. This means exclusion from the home, the severance of all personal
relationships, possibly the loss of employment, and,
should the offender die before reinstatement, the absence
of all the funeral ceremonies which are supposed to benefit
the soul after death. The price which has to be paid for
reinstatement varies a good deal with the offence, and if
the fault be not serious, can be very slight, though it may
be made very heavy for grave breaches of caste duty.

Repeated efforts have been made to modify or eliminate
the caste system from Hinduism. The most notable and
successful was that of Buddha, but in the end the system
proved too strong for the faith which he founded, and only
faint traces of his work remain in India. One of these may
be seen in a custom which obtains in the worship of
Jagannath, one of the gods connected with the Vishnu
group. At his great Temple in Puri, one of the most famous
temples in India, every worshipper, as he enters the
courts, is touched by a "sweeper"—one of the lowest of

all castes. This indicates that within the precincts of the Temple there is no caste, and though in other circumstances contact with a man of that type would bring pollution, here it conveys no stain. Later reformers have broken loose from the system; a typical illustration may be seen in the Brahmo Somaj, a Theistic movement with an eclectic theology, which, under the leadership of Keshab Chandra Sen, came very near to Christianity. But it is hardly possible to-day to speak of the Brahmo Somaj as Hindu, or even as a form of Hinduism. Very interesting is the attempt made by Mahatma Gandhi to bridge the gulf between the caste Hindus and the "untouchables." If the movement is finally successful, it can only tend to the break up of Hinduism as a religious system, for it is so wide and inclusive, and contains so many forms, that the only features that all types of Hindu have in common are the maintenance of caste and the *tabu* on the ox, particularly on its flesh. Ghandi's saintly character and his martyr death have made an impression on India whose effects cannot yet be estimated. But the story of his predecessors in this enterprise suggests that in the long run he will be no more successful than they were, and we may well doubt whether he will win where even Buddha (whom of them all in many ways he most resembled) was ultimately defeated.

# VI.—PHILOSOPHICAL RELIGIONS

WE noted in the last chapter that under a Polytheistic system of religion there was a tendency for thoughtful men to break away from the recognized forms of belief and worship, and to find some satisfaction for themselves. This tendency operates in two directions, the metaphysical and the ethical, and two of the greatest of living religions show how it is possible for this double impulse to drive men away from religion (in the narrow sense of the term) altogether, and to lead them so far that they end in what is practically a new and independent faith. These two are Buddhism, which claims to-day more adherents than any other religion, and Confucianism, which covers not merely the whole of China, but a large element in Japan also.

Buddhism exhibits a combination of the metaphysical and of the ethical tendencies. On the one hand it may be regarded as a logical application of the philosophical principles which are expressed in the Upanishads, and on the other as a revolt from the moral confusion which seems to be inevitable in any Polytheism. Logically there is no room for gods in a Pantheism like that of the Vedanta, and Siddhartha, the founder of Buddhism, bowed to none. To him, as to the Brahman thinkers, there was only a single entity, though this forms so much the background of his thought that there is comparatively little stress upon it. It is rather assumed than stated, and it is impossible to appreciate his teaching until this is recognized as its basis. Nor is stress laid upon the origin of man, for it is maintained that the idea of independent personality

G

is a delusion, and that personal existence itself is unreal.

The student of Buddhism is faced with one serious practical difficulty. While the main outlines of the founder's teachings were well known, and were long handed down by oral tradition, the actual literary monuments of the faith are several centuries later than his time. Two hundred years after his death the Buddhist "scriptures" had not begun to take shape, and there is need of very great care in isolating the primitive elements from the masses of later accretion in which they have been embedded. It is only in recent years that a beginning has been made with the Higher Criticism of the Buddhist literature—the attempt to trace the structure and growth of the books—or even with the textual criticism. But a beginning has been made, especially by a few western students and by fully qualified Japanese scholars, and we may hope for much clearer light on the origin and development of Buddhism in the next few generations.

It is, therefore, somewhat difficult to define the theology of early Buddhism. To use a phrase common in presentations of the Faith "Brahma was dethroned"; if gods existed at all they existed on the same terms as men, and had no more permanent basis of reality. The search for final truth and redemption, therefore, could ignore them, for they also were subject to the same laws and were exposed to the same vicissitudes and fate as the human seeker himself. There is, however, a strenuous insistence on the reign of Law, though room is carefully left for individual choice and action, and some attempt is made to avoid a pure fatalism.

In the absence of any personal object of devotion it might seem to the western student that the religious instinct would inevitably miss its way, and that the result would satisfy neither the human mind nor the human heart. It is true that in later ages this difficulty manifested itself, and that very great changes took place in the general character of the religion. But even at its inception Buddhism achieved a sublime mysticism and a lofty ethic, and offered its followers a salvation from superstition, fear, and the tyranny of pain. It owes its origin to a very practical attempt to meet one of the great needs of the human spirit. The story goes that Siddhartha,[1] a young prince belonging to the Kshattriya caste (i.e. the warrior caste, standing next to the Brahmans), was brought up in his father's palace at Kapila-Vastu, a town in northern India, completely shielded from the sight and knowledge of all sorrow and suffering. When at last the facts came home to him he set himself to discover the means whereby man might escape from suffering. He practised all the methods in favour with the holy men of his day, and surpassed them all in the extent to which he carried his ascetic practices and austerities. These he found to be of no avail; none gave him relief from the problem which weighed upon his soul, and none brought to him enlightenment. Finally abandoning them he gave himself to meditation, and at last the truth broke upon him and he became the Buddha, the Awakened One.

The great discovery is expressed in "the Four Noble Truths." These are:

(1) All personal existence is inextricably bound up with suffering.

(2) All suffering is due to "thirst," i.e. desire.

(3) Suffering can be avoided only when desire is eliminated.

[1] The different names by which the founder of Buddhism is known may need a word of comment. *Buddha* means "the Awakened One," and is applied in Buddhist theology to many others besides the founder. *Gautama* is his family name, *Siddhartha* (Pali *Siddhattha*) his personal name; that by which he is generally indicated in later Buddhism is *Sakyamuni* (the solitary of the Sakyas), a title applied to him alone. With these last two we may compare the use of the two names *Jesus* and *Christ* in Christian theology. Except in speaking of the events of his life in the world, the name *Sakyamuni* will be used through the present chapter.

(4) Desire can be eliminated only by following the "Noble Eightfold Path."

This Eightfold Path is the primary basis of the Buddhist Ethic, and its divisions are:

1. Right views.
2. Right feelings.
3. Right words.
4. Right behaviour.
5. Right mode of livelihood.
6. Right exertion.
7. Right memory.
8. Right meditation and tranquillity.

At first sight it would appear that there is some ambiguity in the use of the word "right," but as a matter of fact the terms are discussed at length in the Buddhist writings, and their general import is clear. In spite of their monastic basis they offer to men the highest and most complete standard of external conduct that has ever been promulgated, except for the type of life and character enjoined in the Sermon on the Mount, and in theory it can hardly be maintained that the Buddhist ideal of conduct falls materially short of the Christian. It is quite possibly the strength of the ethical element in Buddhism which has given to it the very real power which it undoubtedly possesses, for, in its original purity, at any rate, it had certain weaknesses which rendered it unsatisfactory as a universal faith. These appear in the later history of the religion, and are responsible for many changes which have taken place.

Before entering further into the practical effects of the teaching of Sakyamuni, we must glance at the ideal which he set before men. He expressly denied the existence of an Ego. There are five elements which compose that which seems to be personality: material qualities, sensations,

abstract ideas, predispositions or tendencies, and thoughts.
But there is no solid and permanent core round which they
group themselves, and everyone who is enlightened
perceives that reality is to be found only in a succession
of experiences. But this enlightenment is the possession
of the few, and the illusion of personality still remains
for most sentient beings. As there is no Ego, there can be
no reincarnation in the ordinary sense of the word. But
at the same time Buddha inherited and never seems to
have questioned the Hindu doctrine of Karma, though he
was forced to modify it. In its ordinary Hindu form it
simply states that the soul which has lived carried with it
into the next birth the load of action which it has accumulated, and that the whole of each birth is governed entirely
by that which has gone before. Buddha, on the other hand,
could not think of Karma as a personal inheritance, and
was compelled to formulate a theory of reincarnation
along rather different lines. At death, he taught, the
elements which give rise to the illusion of the Ego—the
five "Skandhas"—are dissipated. The actions which have
sprung from them, however, survive, and these have the
power of gathering round them fresh elements, and
making a new illusory personality.

Whilst there is, therefore, no personal continuity
running through the successive lives, there is a connexion,
a chain of being. This involves (since all personal existence
is bound up with suffering) the repeated introduction of
pain into the world, and it is here that Buddha offered
release to humanity. The Eightfold Path has four stages.
The first is that of entrance. When a man has once
definitely pledged himself to follow the Path, the end is
sure. It may be long delayed, and innumerable lives may
yet be in front of him, but in the end he is certain of
salvation. The second stage is reached when the convert
has in front of him only one more life, after that which he
is now living. Before this is entered certain delusions are

eliminated, and during it still further progress is made. The third and fourth stages are those of the man who has entered on his last life; in the former of the two his remaining delusions and desires are overcome, and in the latter he has already attained to perfection and simply awaits death in order to reach the final goal. This state is that of the "Arhat," and is that of Sakyamuni himself during the years between his enlightenment and his death. At death the Arhat passes into what is known as *Nirvana* (Pali *Nibbana*).

The attainment of Nirvana is the ultimate goal set before men by Buddhism. Yet no term in the whole vocabulary of the world's religion has aroused more discussion or is less certain in its meaning. It is indeed probable that Sakyamuni himself used it in more than one sense, adapting his teaching to the particular audience with which he might at any given time be faced. The truth seems to be that he had passed out of the realm of doubt and fear and entered into a wholly new experience. The terror of the world, the fear of pain, the dread of superstition, the threatening clouds of philosophic doubt—all had passed from him, and the relief and revulsion had left him in a state of ecstatic calm for which he could find no positive language. Inexpressibly more restful than joy and more joyful than rest, it paradoxically combined all that was most worth having in both types of happiness— it was a peace that passed all understanding. Thus descriptions of Nirvana are practically always negative, and even so the extent of the negations is somewhat difficult to determine. Sakyamuni himself seems to have described it as the annihilation of thirst, of sorrow, and of rebirth, and to have declined to say whether it meant continued existence of any kind after the physical death of the Arhat. In spite, then, of the praises lavished on it by his followers, it is difficult to escape the conclusion that it involves at least the extinction of personal identity.

The first of the illusions to be conquered on the first stage
of the Path is the illusion of the Self, and though "Self"
may not exactly correspond to the western conception of
personal individuality, it can scarcely be maintained that,
if the road starts here, the ultimate goal is likely to leave
much place for personality as most of us understand it.
A passage from one of the Buddhist classics quoted by
Rhys Davids runs: "They who, by stedfast mind have
become free from evil desire, and well trained in the
teachings of Gautama; they, having obtained the fruit of
the fourth Path, and immersed themselves in that am-
brosia, have received without price, and are in the enjoyment of Nirvana. Their old Karma is exhausted, no new
Karma is being produced; their hearts are free from the
longing after future life; the cause of existence being
destroyed, and no new yearnings springing up within them,
they, the wise, are extinguished like this lamp." Since each
new birth is due to accumulated and effective Karma, a
new birth is impossible, and since there is no connecting
and permanent element in the different births which
might survive the last physical death, strict logic would
demand that the Arhat after death ceases altogether to
exist. Yet Sakyamuni himself strongly condemned the
doctrine of annihilation, and left the paradox unsolved.
To him who has attained the ineffable bliss that Sakyamuni
knew, the distinction between time and eternity is insig-
nificant, and it does not matter whether he is to retain his
happiness for ever, or whether it is to last only as long as
he himself endures.

There seems to be reason to believe, however, that
Sakyamuni offered men other ideals than Nirvana, or,
perhaps, presented different aspects of Nirvana to different
types of mind. To each he offered that which was best
suited to it, and there were many who could not breathe
his mountain air. To them the ideal presented is one of
Paradise, and though this should strictly be only a stage

on the road to the final ideal, there has been a distinct
(though not universal) tendency to regard this as the ideal
itself. In any case Sakyamuni mapped the road, and it was
essentially the road of the moral life. For forty-five years,
according to the ancient traditions, Buddha wandered
up and down northern India, teaching his doctrine to the
disciples whom he gathered and sending them out in turn
to become missionaries of the new faith. He soon found it
necessary to organize his followers, and to make a distinction between those who continued to carry on their usual
occupations and those who devoted themselves to the
spread of truth. Thus arose a double ethic, one adapted to
the laity, the other to the clergy.

The former of these appears in several forms, known as
the five, the eight, and the ten precepts respectively. The
five are the minimum commandments whose observance
is enjoined on every Buddhist, and forbid the taking of life,
theft, adultery, falsehood, and the use of intoxicants. The
eight add to these three more, which may be voluntarily
accepted in a special vow: the eating of unseasonable food
at nights, the wearing of garlands and the use of perfumes,
and the use of any bed other than a mat spread on the
ground. The ten are rather statements of sins, which are
enumerated as follows: taking life, stealing, sexual immorality, falsehood, tale-bearing, abuse, frivolous talk,
covetousness, malice, and scepticism. A carping spirit
might find occasion for criticism in the fact that these
precepts are all prohibitions, but this will not be a serious
difficulty to any student who is prepared to take a
genuinely sympathetic attitude to Buddhism. It is
obvious that, especially if the last three precepts of the
ten be included, we have here a very high moral standard,
and that the appeal of Buddhism to the human conscience
leaves little if anything to be desired.

It goes without saying that the moral standard required
of the Buddhist monk is at least as high as that enjoined

upon the laity. Ten precepts are usually enumerated, and are to be found in the formal vow which every monk takes at his initiation. They resemble the eight binding on the laity, but two extra commands are added, and one or two of the others are more stringent. Monks pledge themselves to abstain from singing, dancing, music, and theatrical performances, and also take a vow of complete poverty. They are permitted only the barest necessities of life, such as their robe, their begging-bowl, and their razor, though there is no objection to the ownership of wealth by the order as a whole or by communities within the order. The position is thus very similar to that of some of the monastic orders found amongst Christians, both in the East and in the West. Instead of the prohibition of adultery, complete celibacy is enforced, and the food regulation confines the monk's meal-time to the space between sunrise and noon. It is curious to notice that in spite of the prohibition of the taking of animal life, there seems to be no objection to animal food under ordinary circumstances; it is indeed recorded that the last meal of which the Buddha himself partook consisted in part of pork.

It will be noticed that in the foregoing sketch there is no mention of two normal features of religion, prayer and atonement. The reason is not far to seek. Prayer involves the conception of a person who can be addressed; Buddhism recognizes no such person, and therefore prayer is impossible. Its place in actual religious life, however, is to some extent taken by meditation. Similarly there can be no atonement in the ordinary sense of the word; there can be no reconciliation between a sinful worshipper and the object of his worship. Sin (in so far as the term can be used in speaking of Buddhism) consists either of a breach of the moral law or in ignorance of the truth. These spiritual weaknesses can be removed only by the sinner's own will and by the simple amendment of his life and thought.

The later history of Buddhism is of some importance to the student of Comparative Religion, for it illustrates the difficulties and dangers which beset an atheistic philosophy, however pure its ethic may be. There are to-day two main branches of Buddhism, the Hinayana ("Little Vehicle"), found in Burmah and Ceylon, and the Mahayana ("Great Vehicle"), which was the form current for many centuries in India, and now embraces the Buddhism of Nepal, Thibet, China, and Japan, though each has peculiarities of its own. Both branches, but especially the Mahayana, illustrate the fundamental weakness of Sakyamuni's teaching. The metaphysical conception of endless change, and the denial of the personal identity and particularity of the human soul, may satisfy the philosophic mind, and there is abundant evidence to show that some men are capable of reaching a high level of mysticism under such doctrines. But the number of these is limited, and the great mass of mankind must have something in their religion which will appeal to their more human instincts. Men cannot readily accept a system which lays down as its first and fundamental doctrine a denial of that which seems most real and certain to a man, his own personality. So, too, he will naturally demand personality in the object of his worship. Even where the higher Pantheism has achieved a genuine mysticism—this is true of Neo-Platonists like Plotinus, as well as of Indian thinkers—its tendency is to personify the object of faith. In the second place men need a more positive ideal than that of Nirvana. Taken at its highest, primitive Buddhism offered men a negation of instinct and of other qualities which go to make up man. To a mind oppressed by an overwhelming sense of the mass of human suffering and by the impossibility of escape from it, such a negation might bring hope of a kind, but in the experience of the normal man pain is to some extent balanced by pleasure, and not a few would shrink from a solution of the great problem of life which relieved men of evil only by depriving them of good also. Hence a double tendency may be observed in the later developments of Buddhism—far more obvious, it is true, in the Mahayana than in the Hinayana sects; on the one hand men tended to find in Buddha, and perhaps in others, a personal object of faith, devotion, and worship, and on the other the ideal of a final attainment of Nirvana lost practical importance in the mind of the average Buddhist as compared with the possibility of bliss or woe in the intermediate states which must intervene before that consummation was achieved. In other words, men concentrated far more on the hope of winning entrance to a heaven and avoiding relegation to a hell in future stages of existence. Nirvana was far away, and not wholly desirable; heavens and hells were close at hand, the one supremely attractive, the other supremely terrible. In a certain sense it is true to say that the inferior elements which Buddhism inherited from early Hinduism proved its salvation, and not only enabled it to survive but to spread over the whole of eastern Asia.

Hinayana Buddhism, however, remained much more philosophical, particularly in Ceylon. Yet even in Ceylon there is a tendency to elevate the Buddha into a god. Figures of him are placed in the temples, and the most famous Buddhist shrine in the world is probably that which was erected over a tooth of the Buddha at Kandy. It is said that the object now preserved there is not original, but there can be no doubt that when the temple was built the relic which it enshrined was believed to be genuine. At the same time there are still left in the practical religion of Sinhalese Buddhism many elements which have survived from the primitive Animism. There is a widespread belief in devils, and the life of the average Sinhalese Buddhist is to some extent affected by the fear of supernatural beings. This is even more strongly marked in Burmese Buddhism, where the practical religion consists to a considerable extent in measures taken to avoid the dangers to which men are subject from devils.

It is, however, in the Mahayana that the greatest changes have taken place, and here the natural passion for a personal object of worship has produced an elaborate theology. Buddhahood was not the exclusive privilege of the first teacher; there are others yet to come. These are named Boddhisattvas, and from a comparatively early period three of them have been recognized and adored, Maitreya, Manjusri, and Avalokitesvara. There are, however, large numbers of others, and the result has been that Northern Buddhism has become a complicated Polytheism in which the members of the Pantheon seem to be connected by some metaphysical relation instead of being members of a great divine family. Thus every Buddha is himself threefold, existing as pure being, existing as the coming Buddha or Boddhisattva, and existing as the Buddha who actually appears in the world. In addition to these, famous saints may be included as objects of worship, and in the various forms which Northern Buddhism takes there must be nearly as many deities as in Hindu theology.

Every country which has embraced Buddhism in its Northern form has developed peculiar features of its own. Thus the religion of Thibet is distinguished from the rest by its belief in "living Buddhas." Like all forms of Northern Buddhism, that of Thibet gives to its higher order of monks the name Lama, and the theory of modern Thibetan Buddhism is that the Grand Lama is a reincarnation of the original Buddha, born again into the world as soon as he dies. There is thus a constant succession of Grand Lamas, each of whom is himself the Buddha returned to earth, and as such may be an object of worship. But Thibetan Buddhism is very catholic in its selection of deities, and in practice it includes in its Pantheon not only the primitive demons, but also numbers of Hindu gods.

Chinese Buddhism is more nearly the type of the Northern school, and while it is in theology polytheistic, it has not the peculiarities which distinguished the religion of Thibet. Next to Buddha himself the most popular deity seems to be a feminine form of Avalokitesvara, named by the Chinese Kuan-Yin, and by the Japanese Kwaimon, and worshipped as the goddess of mercy. Buddhism has necessarily undergone some slight practical modifications in Mongolia, where it is the dominant religion, with the result that a large proportion of the population is in monastic orders.

It is, however, important to observe that throughout the whole history of the Mahayana we have a deeper and a more spiritual ideal. It may well be that the religion has gained rather than lost by its deification of its founder, who has "ascended the empty throne of Brahma." The devotee who "takes refuge in the Buddha, the Church and the Law" attains his objects only by faith—faith regarded as a personal relationship and attitude, not merely as the acceptance of a creed. Amongst the many Buddhas recognized in the modern Mahayana, an important place, especially in Japan, is held by Amitabha, who forms with Mahāsthāmaprapta and Avalokitesvara the greatest of the Buddhist Triads. Connected with his name we have a genuine mystical religion, recognizing a personal object of adoration, and seeking as its highest ideal a state of communion with him. And in general the Mahayana is distinguished by its practical substitution of the Boddhisattva for the Arhat. That is to say, it thinks of the perfect state as being one, not of merely passive bliss, but of active benevolence. The Boddhisattva is essentially one who has attained to practical Buddhahood, but prefers to postpone or cast aside the attainment of Nirvana in all its completeness in order that he may bring the supreme happiness into the lives of others. This doctrine avoids one of the most subtle dangers in all religion, that of making its ideal purely selfish, and for the comparatively low aim of saving one's own soul it substitutes that of satisfying the deepest needs of others.

Japan received Buddhism from China, but, in course of time, certain changes have naturally taken place. The most noteworthy of these is the rise into prominence of a sect which is especially devoted to Amitabha. The name Amitabha has been contracted to Amida, and the sect is distinguished by a doctrine which is wholly alien to the spirit of Buddhism as a whole. This is a belief in justification by faith. Elsewhere the Buddhist believes that he can be saved by acquired merit alone; the Amida doctrine states that man can only be saved by the pure grace of Amida, and that the human share in this salvation consists merely in a man's surrendering himself in faith to the god.

There has been, then, a gradual but marked change in the Mahayana school of Buddhism from the teachings of its Founder, and we can trace the development of a real Polytheism. Naturally this has been accompanied by another. The ideal which the Mahayana (and to some extent the Hinayana also) sets before men is no longer the escape from pain by entry into Nirvana. It is, in fact, doubted by some students whether the average Chinese or Japanese Buddhist has ever heard of Nirvana. Certainly in practical religious thought its place is taken by a doctrine of rewards and punishments, heavens and hells. The ideal, then, is to secure the one and to avoid the other. It is a striking testimony to the intense moral passion of Sakyamuni that, in theory at least, Buddhism has always retained its ethical principles, and nothing but goodness will win heaven and wickedness can only lead to hell. Sin, therefore, is partly to be identified with disregard of the injunctions of conscience, though ritual failures are also included. Atonement, the achievement of the ideal in spite of sin, is to be obtained by good deeds which will

more than counterbalance the evil that a man has done.
Good deeds produce merit, and it is this merit which
takes a man to heaven. The whole theory is mechanical,
for a man must acquire a sufficient store of merit, not
merely to equal the demerit due to his evil deeds, but to
leave a large balance in his favour. If he accumulates more
than he needs for himself, the surplus is available for
others as well. It is a little unfortunate for the credit of
some forms of the Mahayana that men tend to think of
ritual acts as more efficacious in the acquisition of merit
than the moral life.

This leads us to the subject of prayer. As we have seen,
in a pure atheistic Pantheism such as that of Sakyamuni
there can be logically no room for prayer, which is essentially some kind of personal communication between the
worshipper and the object of worship. But with the introduction of real deities prayer again becomes not only
possible but inevitable, and prayers are offered to everyone of the Buddhas, Boddhisattvas, Saints, and other
objects of Buddhist worship. Yet in the popular mind the
thought of communion is seldom prominent, and its place
is taken by the theory that the mere repetition of prayers
—frequently in Sanskrit—or of the sacred formula "Om
mane padme hum" is the most efficacious method known
for the acquisition of merit. An ingenious method of
securing this end is found in Northern Buddhism, and is
apparently to be traced to Thibet. This consists in writing
the prayer on paper and enclosing it in a wheel to which a
handle is attached. Every turn of the wheel is, for merit
purposes, equivalent to a repetition of the prayer, and by
this mechanical means large stores of merit may be
secured. In Thibet, too—and this practice holds good
as far south as Darjiling—prayers are written on flags
which are then placed on poles where the wind can reach
them. Every time the wind blows a repetition of the prayer
is credited to the person who set up the pole, and he may

thus acquire the maximum of value for the minimum of effort. Except for the Amitabha sects, all Buddhists of either school seem to base salvation, the achievement of the religious ideal, purely on human activity.

The combined influence of the metaphysical and of the ethical impulses was responsible in India for Buddhism. In China the same causes were at work, and about the time when the Buddha founded his new religion they made themselves manifest. They were, however, less strikingly effective, partly because the Chinese were late in system-atizing their metaphysics[1] and partly because they were not combined in the same movement. The greatest of Chinese philosophers was Lao-tse, whose work is generally dated about a century before Sakyamuni. His work and theories are obscure to the western reader, mainly because it is difficult to define his essential term *Tao*. This seems to be a universal essence, producing and pervading the whole universe. In itself it is nameless and without qualities, but there springs from it another *Tao* which is knowable and efficient. Lao-tse seems to have distin-guished the two in his mind, and to have concentrated on the latter for purposes of practical religion. The highest virtue was to live in accordance with *Tao*, and this tended to a kind of Quietism, for since the *Tao* effects everything by passivity, the really good man would seek to achieve his ends in the same way. Curious and ineffective as this doctrine seems, it does appear that Lao-tse had grasped the truth that the right way to improve human life and conduct is not to impose regulations from the outside, but to accept a fundamental principle, change the radical

---

[1] I am indebted to Dr. Percy J. Bruce for the following note: "The Kung Philosophy is a very well thought out and sustained system, and it does no more than gather up and give new interpretation to the metaphysics of earlier philosophers. From the time of Confucius downwards there was a whole series of philosophical thinkers, whose writings, the more they are studied, the more they are found to reveal profound metaphysical thought."

character, and let conduct be the natural outcome of the newly-won personality. But he spoke to a world given up to Animism, and in the long run his teaching failed to make any serious impression on the faith of his people, though he himself was and is still honoured as one of the greatest men whom China has ever produced. But the Taoist temples to-day are little more than homes of Animist superstition, and the Taoist priest is practically a magician and a diviner.

The ethical impulse expressed itself mainly in Confucius (Kung-fu-tse), who is justly regarded as the real teacher of China. His views on religion are well known. He did not discard religion as some thinkers in the West did; on the contrary, he was prepared to accept the beliefs commonly held by those about him. But he refused to commit himself to any definite religious views, being content with a practical agnosticism. About the spirits whom men commonly worshipped and feared he knew nothing, or at least was prepared to make no statements. He recognized that there were certain traditional obligations, and enjoined their fulfilment, but his attitude here may have been due to that respect for antiquity which characterized all his thinking. Heaven, standing at the head of the spirits, was a fit object of worship for the Emperor alone; lower men must content themselves with inferior beings. He recognized the fact of sin, as everyone must who admits a personal deity of any kind, but, alone amongst the world's great teachers, doubted the general possibility of atonement. "He who has sinned against Heaven has no one else to whom he can pray" is a saying attributed to him.

It is, of course, by his ethical system that Confucius is best known. It is to be noted, however, that he always laid the main stress on external conduct rather than on the inner springs of action. He thought of the ideal life as the fulfilment of certain mutual obligations which were placed

H

on men by their relations to their fellows. The husband
and the wife had duties to one another, so had the father
and the son, the ruler and his people, the teacher and his
pupil. Even the spirits who were worshipped seem to have
been included in his scheme. In each relationship the ideal
was a mean between two extremes, the inferior must be
neither impudent nor servile in his attitude towards the
superior, the superior must be neither domineering nor
undignified towards the inferior. Deportment was to him
of the highest significance, and his own demeanour in
various circumstances was lovingly remembered and
recorded by his disciples. Confucius had the highest
reverence for antiquity, and his ideal was a return to the
life and standards of the best days of the past. He himself
wrote very little, the only book attributed to him being
a short summary of Chinese history. But he edited a
number of ancient works, and is responsible for the place
that the "Five Classics" hold in the thought of China. In
addition to his own work, the *Tsun-ts'ew*, to which allusion
has already been made, these included the *Yi-king*,[1] a
book of magic, the *Shi-king*, a book of Odes, the *Shu-king*,
a book of history, and the *Li-ki*, a book of ritual. These
last four were edited by him, and their present form owes
probably a good deal to him. The whole collection forms
the sacred literature of China, though it is in no sense an
inspired literature or divine revelation. It does, however,
receive the greatest veneration.

The mere reading of the life and teaching of Confucius
fails to explain to us the immeasurable influence which he
has exerted over his people. His teaching is magnificent,
but it is not religion, and its incompleteness is attested by
the hold that Taoism retained and Buddhism won over
the Chinese mind. It is in his personal character that we

[1] It should be remarked that some authorities believe that this
work was not originally intended to be magical, though it was used
for divination. It may have been rather a treatise on moral, social,
and political questions.

must look for the secret of his power. He impressed his
disciples as the perfectly virtuous man, and they have
succeeded in handing on that impression to later ages.
He was, to quote the words of a modern western appreciation, "a fount of moral energy," and not only China but
the world as a whole has reason to be thankful for the
appearance of such a man in a country like China.

# VII.—MONOTHEISM

We have been concerned hitherto with what we may call the normal development of religious belief. We have seen how it is possible to trace back all religions that we know to an Animistic stage, and how from that the usual progress is, sometimes through Polydæmonism, sometimes more directly, to Polytheism. This last form of religion is always in a state of unstable equilibrium. On the one hand there are demands of the human spirit which make it necessary to meet both the moral and the intellectual elements in man's being, and a metaphysic and an ethic gradually appear. As a rule these are found to be inconsistent with the theory and practice of Polytheism, and either they formally break away from it, or we have the phenomenon of two kinds of faith living side by side under the same name and system, yet with comparatively little interaction. Each individual, for his own personal faith, turns to one or to the other, and the actual religion of the cultured classes is a very different thing from that of the great majority. On the other hand, Polytheism in the popular mind never wholly rids itself of its Animistic background; fresh spirits are raised to the rank of deities, and all carry with them traces of their origin. Hence, while the philosophic and cultured minds develop more and more fully a noble system of thinking and conduct— which nevertheless tends to stand aloof from ordinary religion, the popular belief drifts back towards the old Animism, and, though formally rising above it, is in practice largely dominated by belief in, and fear of, nameless and indeterminate spirits.

The philosophy, too, holds its ground with difficulty, at least as long as it remains aloof from a more personal creed. Historically it has nearly always been either fully Pantheistic or at least impersonal. In such doctrines as those of Stoicism and original Buddhism there is no room logically for *worship*, and ordinary men must have that above them to which they can offer personal tribute, whether of fear or of love. It is in Mahayana Buddhism that this tendency is better illustrated than anywhere else, and we have seen how the personality of Sakyamuni and of other Buddhas in various forms has captured the imagination and won the adherence of millions. Buddhism came into existence as a philosophy, but has become a religion.

The same religion presents us with another tendency, appearing most strongly in the Japanese form of the worship of Amitabha, which is yet not fully developed, even there. This is the denial of all objects of worship save one, and the concentration, not merely of worship but also of theology, on a single deity. There are forms of belief in which numbers of gods may be recognized as existing and as being valid in themselves, but the human unit in religion, whether an individual or a whole community, deals with only one. When the choice is personal or temporary the name used to indicate such a belief is *Henotheism* or *Kathenotheism*. Thus there are hymns both in the Vedic literature and in that of Babylon which are addressed to a single god and exalt him as being the sole or at least the supreme god, though each religion as a whole recognizes many others. Where the choice is that of a community—city, tribe, or nation—and is theoretically permanent, the term used is *Monolatry*, and its best examples (perhaps there are no others) are to be seen amongst the more primitive Semitic communities. In Mesopotamia and some other parts of the Semitic world, notably Ugarit, the course of political history and the

genius of poets and theologians so combined these separate
worships that in the historic literature they formed a
Pantheon, though the monolatrous basis is still per-
ceptible, but most of the western and southern Semites,
being politically centrifugal rather than centripetal,
retained their local and tribal deities to a much later
period.

Twice in human history the fuller doctrine which we
call *Monotheism* has developed. This not merely confines
worship to an individual deity, but denies that any other
exists at all. Such spiritual beings as are recognized belong
to a different order, and, whether they be good (angels)
or whether they be evil (devils), are intermediate in status,
power, and nature between God and man, approximating
rather to the latter. It now becomes possible to speak of
God, not of gods, for He is viewed as an individual, not
as a specimen of a species. Monotheism differs again from
Pantheism in its insistence on personality. Whilst not
necessarily denying to God all the attributes of a metaphysical ultimate, it insists that personality must be
included amongst them, and finds that though it is possible
to regard God as Causation, Righteousness, Love, Truth
(not merely causative, righteous, loving, or true), yet for
purposes of practical religion it is God as a Person with
whom man has to deal. Thus God stands as an individual
over against every human individual, and that same line
which parts one human being from another parts him also
from God. There may be (and in all known forms of
Monotheism there is) a similarity between human personality and divine, but there is no continuity of essence.
Men may have something in them which they call divine,
inasmuch as it can appreciate and respond to the divine
approach and appeal, but they are not parts of God, nor
are they elements in His being. Four Monotheistic religions
are known: Zoroastrianism, which, in spite of the labours
of scholars during the last generation is still somewhat

obscure, Judaism, Islam, and Christianity, of which the third and fourth are direct descendants of the second and derived from it their monotheistic basis. It is to be remarked that all four have a conspicuous ethical element, though this is not equally developed in all of them, being weakest in Islam and strongest in Christianity.

Zoroastrianism takes its name from its founder, the Persian Zarathustra, who was probably a contemporary of Ezekiel. The earlier religion of Persia was a Polytheism of the usual Indo-European type; that is to say, the gods are thoroughly individual and were originally nature spirits personified and raised to the rank of "high gods." Its differences from Vedic religion were inconsiderable, and some of the gods, notably the sun-god Mithra, survived independently alongside of the new faith. But there had been time enough to allow of divergence in the use of terms which were originally common to both India and Persia, the best instance being the change of value undergone by the two terms Deva and Asura (Iranian Dæva and Ahura). Originally these seem to have been classes of gods which were on an equality, but in India the former name was applied to the gods of light and goodness, while the latter were degraded to the level of demons. In Iranian religion the opposite change took place, and it was the Dævas who degenerated, the Ahuras who rose to full deity.

The principal source for our knowledge of Zoroastrianism is the literature known as the Zend-Avesta. Repeated persecutions have mutilated the collection, and it is generally recognized that it is imperfect as it now exists amongst the Parsis, who are the modern adherents of Zoroastrianism. Even in the extant books it is possible to trace several strata, the earliest of which consists of hymns called the Gathas, and these are generally supposed to represent most nearly the teaching of Zarathustra himself.

The name given to God in the Gathas is Ahura Mazda,

literally Wisdom of Ahura. It looks as though there were
some intermediate stage which we can no longer recover
between this and the earlier Iranian theology. There may
have been a real philosophical development comparable
to that which took place in India before the time of
Zarathustra. The teacher himself is depicted as a simple
shepherd, and whilst it is not impossible that he should
have elaborated such a conception as that of Ahura
Mazda, it seems unlikely, unless there were some philosophical speculation lying behind him. For his creed is
not a simple elevation of one of the deities of a Pantheon
to a unique position, such as the attempt made by Akhen-
Aton to make Aton the supreme and indeed the only god
of Egypt; it is the deification of an abstract principle
which may be supposed to have been originally an attribute of more than one god. Hence we may conjecture that
the development of these divine attributes and their
recognition in one or more of the members of the Iranian
Pantheon was earlier than Zarathustra himself. The
impression is borne out by the fact that we are told of
another order of beings, lower indeed than Ahura Mazda,
but higher than man. These are, in the Gathas, six in
number, and are named the Amesha Spentas. Like Ahura
Mazda himself, they derive their names from qualities
which may be ascribed to personality, human or divine,
and later Zoroastrian theology elevated them to the
rank of subordinate gods. To Zarathustra they were
probably not more than divine qualities, Truth, Good
Thought, Dominion, Piety, Health, and Immortality. But
he seems also to have recognized numberless other
spirits, good and evil, angelic and diabolical. We may,
perhaps, see in these the reduced forms of others of the
old Aryan deities, for many of them bear names which
can be paralleled from the Vedic Pantheon. Over against
Ahura Mazda stands the great spirit of evil, Angra Maiyu,
later called Ahriman. The two are nearly equal in power

and wage unending war on one another, but it does not seem that there is any real dualism, for the ultimate victory of the Good is assured.

Zoroastrianism presents a clear picture of a life after death, either of bliss or of suffering, and the enjoyment of the former and the avoidance of the latter constitute the chief ideal of the religion. Sin is in some of its forms the violation of the moral law of conscience, and in this connection the religion has developed a high standard of morality. But, at any rate in the later religion, it is still more the incurring of ceremonial uncleanness, of which the worst form, at least in modern Parsiism, is contact with a dead body. Since a peculiar sanctity attaches alike to earth and fire, bodies must be neither buried nor burnt, but are exposed to be devoured by vultures. Sacrifice seems to play little part in religious practice, but prayer at the fire-temples is valuable and important. The main road, however, to the Zoroastrian heaven is the path of an upright moral life, free alike from ethical wrongdoing and from ceremonial uncleanness.

Like most other religions which look back to a noble historical founder, Zoroastrianism does not seem to have maintained its theological simplicity. It developed in Persia itself, and even there it does not seem to have preserved its monotheistic purity. Cyrus, in his inscriptions, uses the language of the ordinary polytheist, and though Darius I ascribes his victories and his throne to Ahura Mazda, he speaks of him in the same terms as, for instance, Sennacherib uses of Asshur, and may even have held him to be his personal choice amongst many other possible deities. Both he and his successors on the Persian throne even went so far as to claim deity themselves in Egypt, and to recognize the other gods of that country. Without attempting to trace the history of the religion through its many vicissitudes, we may note that there seems to have been in recent years a definite movement towards reform, with a distinct tendency to revert to the teaching of Zarathustra himself. The higher Criticism of the Zend-Avesta has done much to make this possible, and it may well be that in Zoroastrianism we shall in the next few generations have one of the purest forms of Monotheism that the world has known. Whilst the official religion does not appear to leave much room for the cultivation of direct personal relations with Ahura Mazda, a high degree of mysticism is possible to the more enlightened members of the Parsi community, and it seems that in some ways the religion is learning something from Christianity. Its great weakness would appear to be the insignificance or even absence of any clear or positive doctrine of an atonement. Sin can be expiated only by a corresponding balance of righteous acts, and sooner or later it must become clear that this does not suffice to promote the ideal moral relations between the worshipper and the object of his devotion. In the long run a heaven that can be secured by external conduct cannot prove a satisfactory final ideal for the human spirit.

Zoroastrianism sprang from a typical Aryan Polytheism. The other great Monotheism is that which was developed by Israel, and broke away at a point lower down in the scale of religious evolution. There is no religion whose history we can trace with more clearness, for we have literature coming from practically all except the very earliest period. We may distinguish four distinct stages:

A. Before the conquest of Palestine.
B. From the conquest of Palestine to about 750 B.C.
C. From about 750 B.C. down to the Exile.
D. Exilic and Post-exilic religion.

It is true that these merge into one another, and that the characteristic features of each have their roots in that which preceded it, whilst it must not be assumed that progress was evenly distributed throughout the whole people. But for a rough division, stressing the main tendencies, this arrangement will suffice.

Of the religion of Israel before the conquest—that is, during the nomad period of her history—we know comparatively little. Probably the religion was of the ordinary type to be seen elsewhere amongst Semitic nomads. They lived in a world peopled by spiritual beings, to whom the general name of El was given, and one amongst these Elim was recognised as the tribal or national God of Israel. His name was Yahweh, and His home was in the far south, in the country that lay between Palestine and Egypt or between Palestine and northern Arabia. The exact spot is uncertain; there are two traditions, one of which locates Him in Sinai (possibly near Kadesh Barnea, the modern Ain Kadis), the other in Horeb, which is frequently supposed to have lain to the east of the Gulf of Akaba. His place in the tribe was that usually assigned to the national El, except for one distinction which is fundamental. Whilst other peoples regarded their gods as natural members of the tribe, and could give no account of the way in which the human and the divine first came into contact, the Israelites traced their religion back to a definite historical starting-point. There is no reason to doubt the truth of the statement that they were first introduced to Yahweh by Moses, who had led them, or some of them, out of Egypt to the sacred mountain, and that there they entered into a solemn covenant with Yahweh, who thereupon became their God, as they became His people. Now the term rendered "covenant" does not necessarily imply a bargain as it might do in normal speech. Its essence is the unification of two parties into a single entity. Conditions might be imposed by one side or the other or by both, but a covenant relation was possible without any conditions on either side. The unification might be valid only within a limited sphere or it might be complete, whether there were conditions

or not. In the case of Israel and Yahweh terms are laid
on the people, but none are accepted by the Deity. It is,
of course, open to Him to break the union if He sees fit,
and Israel automatically breaks it in failing to observe
any of the accepted conditions. Thus the religion of Israel
started with a definite act of union, voluntarily offered by
Yahweh and voluntarily accepted by Israel. He had
existed without them, and could dispense with them if
the "covenant" were broken, and it is significant that one
of the epithets which the Israelite saint applied to Yahweh
was "covenant-keeping." As to His moral character we
have little evidence, but that little goes to show that He
was endowed with the ordinary good—and bad—qualities
of the Semitic nomad. He appears as fierce and blood-
thirsty at times, but in certain ways demands a high
standard of conduct. Nomad ethics are usually high, for
the very life of the people depends on the purity of its
blood, and the practical absence of private property
relieves men of the great majority of the temptations
which invade the more elaborate social order of agriculture, commerce, and industry.

Details of the relations between God and man in
nomadic Israel are very obscure. But it is clear that the
people had some portable emblem, or rather vehicle, of
Yahweh which could move with them on their wanderings,
and was believed to contain His actual presence. This was
almost certainly the so-called Ark, a box which was said
to contain two stones received on the sacred mountain at
the time of the original covenant. Later ages believed that
the terms of the covenant were inscribed upon them, but
the earlier view is that the Ark was the actual residence
of a very powerful personality. It had, of course, a tent of
its own, and attendants, whose duty it was to perform any
services that were required, and to interpret the will of
Yahweh to His people when they made inquiry. The
method which they adopted for ascertaining the will of

Yahweh may have been some form of the sacred lot, but the great majority of the questions addressed to them by private Israelites presumably sprang out of disputes, and they would have to guide them, not merely the general ethical principles which all Israelites recognized, but also a growing body of legal decisions. They would also be responsible for the care of the Ark and all that was connected with it when the people were moving from one encampment to another, or were taking the Ark with them into battle.

In thinking of the human side of the religion, it is important to remember that in early Israel, as in most other primitive peoples, the unit was not the individual man or woman but the community as a whole. Separate persons were related to Yahweh, not independently, but as elements in the whole nation. If one man sinned the whole of Israel sinned, and must in some way expiate their wrongdoing, or all the people would suffer. Similarly the reward for conduct especially pleasing to Yahweh fell on others in addition to the man whose acts had won His favour. Thus, when prayer was offered—and though we have no direct evidence we may suppose that it was—it was offered on behalf of the whole people, though it does not seem that there could be any general worship in the sense in which it was later developed. It is still a moot point as to whether there was any such institution as sacrifice. Some of our earliest authorities (the great prophets of the eighth and seventh centuries) appear to deny it altogether, but on the other hand it is difficult to imagine an early people maintaining a religion in which there was no sacrifice, and the festival of the Passover, which involved sacrifice, was almost certainly earlier than the conquest of Palestine. New Moons and Sabbaths may have been observed, but if that were so, then the Sabbath is more likely to have been a monthly festival of the full moon than a weekly day of rest.

The ideal relations between Yahweh and His people were those in which He was able or was induced to satisfy their material needs. These, clearly, were simple, and consisted mainly in right guidance to the best supplies of water and pasture, and in defence against enemies. In most such early communities, the God is thought to be whimsical and capricious, but a most powerful friend when kept in a good humour. Sin might be either a breach of the simple moral law of which Yahweh was the guardian (rules mainly affecting sexual relations and the life of members of the tribe), a direct insult to His personality of such as the breach of an oath taken in His name, or the violation of some *tabu*, general or occasional. It seems that for the community there was no means of atonement except by the elimination from its midst of the offending member, either by death or by expulsion. The mode of execution was probably stoning, which would avoid direct physical contact between the executioner and the criminal.

The conquest of Canaan produced radical changes in the popular religion. Israel came into contact with an agricultural people, possessing a civilization a good deal more developed than her own, and a religion which matched their social development. At bottom the ideas of deity were not dissimilar; the objects of worship were spiritual beings only slightly differentiated, and with few personal names. The generic name was Ba'al, and the Ba'al differed from the El mainly in being an agricultural "god," a fertility-spirit. His primary function was the care of the ground and the production of the typical crops, corn, grapes, olives, flax. Instead of being attached to a wandering tribe, he was bound down to a locality, and had little or no influence outside his own fixed home.

The means whereby the Ba'als entered into contact with man included those which we have learnt to recognize as normal. It was believed that there were places and occasions especially suitable to "theophany," and that

from time to time the divine beings might appear to men
in recognizable physical guise. There were also the priests,
and, though we have little or no direct evidence on the
subject, we may assume with some security that these
officials were concerned, not only with the acceptance of
offerings and with the regulation of worship, but also with
divine communications with man. No doubt there were
secular judges, but it may be taken for granted that
disputes and other questions would be brought to the
sanctuary for settlement, and that in many cases the will
of the god would be made known through the priests.

But we have in Palestine, and also in Asia Minor, a
phenomenon which, as far as we know, appeared nowhere
else in the early world. Certainly no traces have yet been
found in Europe, Mesopotamia, Arabia, or Egypt, except
such as can be proved to have been imported from the
coast-lands of the eastern Mediterranean. This peculiar
feature was the inspired ecstasy to which the name
"prophecy" (in a narrow sense) was given. It becomes a
frequent feature in the later religion of Israel, but we have
evidence of its existence in Syria before the coming of the
Hebrews into the country. Its outward manifestations
consisted in a strange seizure, in which the limbs might be
violently moved, or on the other hand the muscles might
be constricted as to produce a state resembling catalepsy.
The subject was "possessed" by a supernatural power, and
what he said and saw was attributed directly to divine
sources. The condition might be induced at will by the use
of drugs, and persons liable to it were also affected by
music. It tended to work on groups rather than on individuals, and carried with it a certain contagion; if men
came into contact with a group of ecstatics, they too might
be similarly inspired. In general it was distinguished from
the priesthood by being irregular and theoretically
unofficial.

Worship was far more elaborate than in the earlier

stages of development. Every town and considerable village had its "high place," a solid building or group of buildings erected at some convenient spot near the town, usually on an elevated site above it. This sanctuary was sometimes a large one, and, as far as our evidence goes, contained a great many smaller rooms besides the main chamber in which the god was thought to have his dwelling. Some of these would be used by the attendant priests, others were at the disposal of the worshippers. The central act of worship was sacrifice, which had two forms. In one of these the victim was cooked and eaten by the worshipper, the blood and internal fat being presented at the altar, and a portion of the flesh reserved for the priests. The sacrifice thus became a communion meal, in which god and worshipper shared. In the other form the whole of the victim was withdrawn from the use of the worshipper and became the property of the god. Here again we have diversity of practice; some victims were burnt whole upon the altar, others were eaten by the priests, always excepting the blood and internal fat, which remained the actual portion of the god. The latter type of sacrifice obviously has nothing of the idea of communion in it, and becomes primarily a gift to the god.

It may be taken for granted that certain dues were held to be the property of the god, especially portions of the fruits of the soil. These naturally took the form of tithes and firstfruits, a tribute paid to the god in recognition of his ownership of the land and of his activities in promoting fertility. There were also great festal seasons, and the ritual connected with them may have its origin partly in ideas which resemble those underlying the practices of sympathetic magic. Thus the greatest of the festivals took place at the beginning of the agricultural year, in the autumn, when men were about to start preparing the ground in readiness for the new seed. Some scholars suppose that the ritual here was essentially sexual, simulating

and assisting the fertilizing of the crops; the best evidence
is to be found in the Adonis festival of northern Syria and
Phœnicia. Closely parallel is the ritual whose myth has
recently become known to us through discoveries at Ras
Shamra. Here we have the stress laid on the dying and
rising god which symbolises the revival of dead nature in
the spring. Another important point in the year came with
the cutting of the first ears of corn in the spring (the
harvest in Palestine begins to ripen in March or April).
The introduction of the new crop was attended with
dangers, especially that of contamination, which might
have crept into the old foodstuffs during the year, and
we may guess that during this festival the use of leaven
(i.e. sour dough) was prohibited. The third festival came
some seven weeks later, at the natural conclusion of the
corn harvest. All three were occasions of great rejoicing,
when the grim toil of the agricultural life was relaxed,
and men gave themselves up to freedom and, possibly, to
licence.

Sin, in such a religion as this, may be either the omission
of rites or the violation of *tabus*. There is no strongly moral
conception of deity; on the contrary, the conditions of the
great festivals tended to produce the opposite result, and
it seems to be beyond doubt that actions which would be
strongly condemned in private life were not merely
tolerated but enjoined in worship. In other words, secular
ethics stood on a higher plane than religious morality, and
the god was not greatly interested in human conduct
except in so far as it directly touched him. Atonement,
however, was frequently necessary, and this was secured
by sacrifice of the second class, that in which the victim
was wholly given up by the worshipper, though the greater
part of it might become the food of the priests. The atonement may thus have been a form of fine or attempt to
purchase the divine favour, though it is possible that there
were animistic or even magical features in the ritual of

Atonement, and that a special efficacy attached to the blood of the slaughtered animal. We know that this was so in Israel, but we lack direct evidence which would prove the earlier Canaanite ritual to have involved the application of sacrificial blood to the altar. This element in the rules of sacrifice may have been apotropaic, or it may have symbolized in Israel the renewal of the ancient covenant, and the re-introduction of the worshipper into the true relation with Yahweh. But the fact of atonement through sacrifice is attested by numerous inscriptions which have come down to us from agricultural Semitic communities.

The first effect on Israel of the passage from the nomadic to the agricultural stage seems to have been a very strong tendency to abandon their old worship and adopt that of the new civilization on which they were entering. Indeed it seems likely that they accepted the whole of the Canaanite culture, including its social customs, law, mythology, and religion. This is the best way to account for the similarities between the culture of Israel and that of Babylonia, which, we have reason to believe, was the chief element underlying that of pre-Israelite Palestine. There were strong reasons for this course. Yahweh was a storm and a wilderness god; His familiarity with the operations of agriculture was more than doubtful. Further, the Ba'als, if neglected, might prove dangerous. The land was theirs by immemorial prescription, and if their lordship were not fully recognized calamity might follow. But during the period between the conquest and the monarchy it became clear, to the best minds at least, that neglect of Yahweh was disastrous. For the Israelites formed only small settlements in the midst of higher and more developed communities, and the imperative need for them was that of unity. They were isolated, with broad belts of enemies separating their main centres, and the only unifying force they had was their religion. Even their language seems to have been abandoned in favour of that already current

in Palestine though it contributed a number of words to
the vocabulary.

The second stage, therefore, was one of *Syncretism*, a
combination of two religions, in which the forms of the
one were preserved with the terminology of another, and,
perhaps, with some of its features added. Thus Israel
retained the name of Yahweh, and seems to have combined with the agricultural spring festival its ancient
nomad celebration of the Passover, which naturally fell
about the same time. In other respects she seems to have
kept the Canaanite forms of worship. She recognized
Yahweh as the only God for her, but He was now an
agricultural God, and needed therefore to be worshipped
as other agricultural gods had been. Ritual formerly
employed in the service of the Ba'als was now appropriate
to Him, and, as the names of some of the most devoted of
Yahweh enthusiasts show, Israel even gave Him the title
of Ba'al. In short, Yahweh became a Ba'al.

This was the general position down to the middle of the
eighth century, perhaps complicated by the importation
of foreign cults owing to commerce or conquest and by
the survival of some ancient forms of religion. At the same
time there were branches of Israel which had remained in
the nomad or semi-nomad stage. In the east and the south
the soil and climate made agriculture practically impossible, and men retained their old ways, their simpler
religion, and their purer ethic. Yet they felt themselves
to be a part of Israel, and to be associated with the same
God. From time to time efforts were made from the
wilderness to purify religion or to revert to the nomad life,
and we can see something of the interaction of the two
social orders in such groups as the Rechabites and in such
individuals as Elijah.

It is the mention of this last name which really introduces us to the third stage in the development of the
religion of Israel. Elijah comes from the eastern wilderness,

and has a double protest to make. The first element in his message is a condemnation of the foreign worship of the Tyrian Ba'al, introduced by Jezebel, and here he may well have had the whole of popular feeling behind him. The second is the condemnation of social injustice, as manifested in the treatment of Naboth by Jezebel. Elijah, as a Prophet, was an enthusiast for Yahweh, and the religion of Yahweh, as he had known it, had no room for either of these things.

The tendency thus adumbrated in Elijah appears still more clearly in his great successors, the canonical prophets of the eighth century. Amos, Hosea, Micah, and Isaiah all denounced social injustice which was rampant in central Palestine, both north and south, and the moral iniquities with which worship was associated. They recognized the evils and the perils of the agricultural civilization as clearly as did the Rechabite, but their remedy was not economic but religious. They bade people seek Yahweh Himself apart from all the elaboration of professional worship, and apply to their life the principles involved in His ascertainable will. They presented Him as a God of nature, who was responsible for the creation and the maintenance of the physical world. They thought of Him as the God of History, whose plan for humanity was responsible for all national and international movements. Even the great racial migrations were under His control, and not merely Israel, but also other nations, owed their position to Him. Above all, He was the God of universal morality, who claimed from all men and from every race righteousness. For the first time the demands of conscience was supported by those of religion, even identified with them; sacrifice and ritual were declared to be futile and, indeed, contrary to the will of Yahweh. His primary requirement was that men should appreciate His moral character and strive to imitate it in their dealings with their fellows. In Amos the stress is laid on social justice;

in Hosea on a deeper quality, to which, for want of a better term, we may give the name Love; in Isaiah on a personal and national consecration to Yahweh Himself as a supremely ethical God.

It may appear that these doctrines necessarily carried with them a full and genuine Monotheism. But though, in combination with a strict Monolatry, they would ultimately lead to Monotheism, it does not follow that the pre-exilic Prophets realized the implications of their own beliefs. The doctrine of creation, for instance, was one which was widely held amongst the nations, and each attributed the work to its own deity. Thus similar stories of creation seem to have been common to the mythology of the whole of Mesopotamia, but whereas in early times in the far south the Creator was identified with the Sumerian god Enlil, the Babylonian form of the story makes Marduk the author of the world, and the Assyrian mythologist substitutes his god Asshur. It is quite possible that the Hebrew Prophets thought of Yahweh as supreme —here they seem to have accepted views which were already in existence in Israel—and that other divine or semi-divine beings were really subordinate to Him. It would be precarious to assume a true Monotheism in Israel at all till after the destruction of Jerusalem in 585.

The seventh century saw another group of Prophets, all of whom lived in the generation that saw the end of the monarchy. Of the four who are usually assigned to this period (Zephaniah, Nahum, Habakkuk, and Jeremiah), the most important are the last two. Habakkuk was the first, as far as we know, to ask the baffling and yet fruitful question, "If Yahweh is the righteous governor of the universe, why does He allow wickedness to prosper and righteousness to lead to disaster?" Such a question could have been asked only on the basis of a doctrine of a righteous God, but when once that view was accepted it was bound to arise, and the best minds in Judaism and

Christianity have sought for a valid answer. Jeremiah's contribution to the world's religious thinking was of a different kind. His experiences were such as to lead him to stand apart from his people and alone with his God, and the result of his bitter agony of spirit is to be seen in the slow yet real growth of individualism in religion. It was no longer true that the individual man met God only through the community; he had also to deal with Him personally, as one over against another. Each must suffer for his own sins, and each must be saved by his own righteousness—a doctrine which, whilst it finds more emphatic expression in Ezekiel, nevertheless seems to go back to Jeremiah.

With the Exile we enter on the fourth stage in the evolution of the Jewish faith. That disaster proved in the long run to be perhaps the greatest spiritual experience through which any nation has passed. Israel still held the old territorial view of Yahweh, and she went to Babylon believing that she had left behind her not only her home and country, but also her God. And she found Him in Babylon. The maintenance of prophecy and other features of the deeper spiritual life of Israel, in spite of the distance from the central home of Yahweh, tended to show her that He was indeed universal, and the treatment that the gods of Babylon received at the hands of Nabuna'id towards the end of the Exile clinched the matter for her. In the utterances of the great unknown Prophet whom we date at the close of the Exile (Isa. xl–lv), we have for the first time the proclamation of a clear and uncompromising Monotheism. Yahweh is God; there is no other.

It is from this position that the religious life of the post-exilic period develops. But we have no longer a single thread that we can trace with clearness like that which we have followed during the pre-exilic period. Four lines may be detected, and though they interacted on one another, yet they can best be understood apart. The first of them is the development of Law. The conception of Scripture—that is, of divine revelation through literature —goes back to the promulgation of the Book of Law (generally, though not universally, identified with Deuteronomy or a part of it) discovered in the Temple in 621 B.C. It was developed later, and civil and ceremonial practices, many of them no doubt ancient, were included in an elaborate code which now forms the greater part of the books from Exodus to Numbers. The interpretation and the observance of this Law became one of the leading characteristics of the later Judaism, and gave rise to a whole profession, that of the Scribes. It was a feature of religion which was not and could not be destroyed with the Temple, and it remains the chief preoccupation of the orthodox and pious Jew to this day.

Alongside of it there sprang up a religion of the Synagogue. The centralization of sacrifice in the days of Josiah had made it necessary for men to find some other expression of their religious life, and in the local communities there arose forms of public worship in which sacrifice had no part. Men found it possible to meet God and to enjoy the full sense of mystical communion with Him without the elaborate Temple ritual, and some of the most exquisite of our later Psalms seem to owe their inspiration to the life of the Synagogue and not to that of the Temple. There thus developed an inner sense of God, a genuine saintliness, which survived, because it could dispense with, all outward forms and all material symbols. Men learnt to stand alone with God, and to know Him as a person, an unseen but loving Friend.

In the third place we have a philosophy. It is true that no Semitic people ever cultivated largely the metaphysical mind, but still men did ask questions about the being of God, His methods in creation and His modes of entering into human life. Impressed by the power manifested in the universe, they spoke of God's Word as His efficient agent;

amazed by the intelligence displayed in the structure of the world, they found in Him the vital, almost personal quality of Wisdom. In the later Jewish thought, especially as it came into contact with the mind of Greece, we have these conceptions developed, and Jewish philosophy reaches its highest point in the Book of Wisdom and in Philo of Alexandria.

The fourth line of thought was eschatology. This had two sides, a personal and a general, and again, though the two in practice were intertwined, they sprang from different roots. Man finds it almost impossible to believe that death ends his existence, and even in early times the Israelite had had some vague notion of a continuation of life even after death. But it was a continuation either in the grave where his body was bestowed or in a vast underground realm where he was cut off from all that made life worth living, cut off indeed from Yahweh Himself. When men began seriously to discuss the problem first raised by Habakkuk, they sought to find various solutions which would offer a readjustment on earth. To the writers of Ps. xxxvii and of the Book of Job the whole drama of religion must be played on the stage of this life, and recompense and punishment must find their expression before death. This was clearly sometimes impossible, and the Book of Job is concerned with a situation in which such a solution, though adopted in the popular theology typified by the three friends, was obviously out of the question. Through his struggles the poet works his way to another solution. Since this life leaves him in moral confusion, there must be some means whereby justification can be secured after death. Before the poem is ended Job finds a certain rest in the conviction that after death he will see God, and will be justified by Him. The writer of Ps. lxxiii seems to be led by a similar train of thought to a like conclusion, but the idea did not seem to take any strong hold on the popular mind till the middle of the second century B.C. The persecution of Antiochus Epiphanes cut off multitudes of pious and faithful Jews; their brethren rose in revolt and in the end won religious and political freedom. But it was not just that those who had suffered should be shut out from the triumph, and so men came to believe that they too would live again. The doctrine of the resurrection as formulated by these early Pharisees may appear to us crude and materialistic, for they believed in the literal return of the body to earth, and had not risen to the purer Greek conception of personality surviving all material form, and enduring as incorporeal spirit through eternity. But it is to be noted that everywhere else a doctrine of the life after death arose apart from religion, being based either on certain natural analogies, as in the so-called "Mystery Religions," or on philosophical psychology. The Jewish doctrine sprang directly out of religion, out of what the Israelite believed the character of God to be, and out of what he knew to be his relationship with that God. It finds its noblest and its simplest statement in the teaching of Jesus Himself, who held that God, as He presented Him, could never allow a physical event like death to interfere with a genuine spiritual communion between the Heavenly Father and His earthly child.

The general eschatology is more complicated, and centres round two main ideas, those of the Kingdom of God and of the Messiah. From very early times men had believed that when things grew too bad to be mended—eschatology always flourishes in times of distress—God would interfere, bring the present order to an end, and inaugurate a new world in which His will should be supreme. We cannot trace this thought through all its development from the days of Amos onwards—and Amos found it a popular belief—down to the end of the second Temple, but it played a more important part in the religious thinking of the Jew of the first century B.C. and of the first century A.D. It took various forms, and we have a whole literature which deals with it. To this type of writing the name Apocalypse is usually given, and two Apocalyptic books are found in our Bibles, the Book of Daniel in the Old Testament and the Book of the Revelation (which, though Christian in its present form, seems to have been based on Jewish apocalyptic writings) in the New Testament. Others appear under the names of great heroes of the Hebrew past. Thus we find them under such names as Ezra, Baruch, Isaiah, Moses, and others, while there is a whole library which carries the name of Enoch. Sometimes these present the new Kingdom as earthly, sometimes as heavenly, but there is always a time of dire calamity preceding its inauguration. Miraculous events occur, and the wicked are overwhelmed, sometimes to perish utterly, sometimes to endure an eternity of torment in hell, but the righteous always survive, either in earth or in heaven, and share in the triumph of their God.

In some forms of Apocalypse a limited period of happiness on earth precedes the final judgement and the establishment of the heavenly Kingdom. There is usually a strong nationalistic element in the predictions, for the wicked generally include the heathen, especially such heathen nations as have oppressed Israel. It is noticeable that a universalist tone, which is manifest at a few points in the history of Jewish thought, practically disappears in apocalyptic literature.

In some forms of eschatology, though not in all, a Messiah appears. As far back as Isaiah we can trace the expectation of an ideal king who should rule over Israel as a king ought to rule, in perfect justice and in perfect love. The conception reappears sporadically in Hebrew writings, and takes clear shape in some of the Apocalypses of the second century B.C. and onwards. Again, there are wide differences of presentation. Sometimes the Messiah is the agent used by God for the closing of the old age and the introduction of the new; sometimes he appears only when the victory is won. Sometimes he reigns as the vice-gerent of God on earth, sometimes in heaven. Once, and once only, as far as the literature is yet known to us, he is not human but divine.

Here, then, we have a picture of the Judaism of the first century A.D., especially as it survived the destruction of the second Temple and the end of the Jewish state. For the Sadducee movement perished with the fall of Jerusalem; it was Phariseeism that lived on in the Rabbis. That which was permanent in Judaism was a clear pure Monotheism, with a strong moral content, a real and deep spiritual life, a powerful sense of sin, mainly moral, an atonement through sacrifice or, later, through prayer, fasting, and almsgiving, and a great hope that some day the cause of God would be vindicated, and His will done, as in heaven, so on earth.

# VIII.—ISLAM

THERE are to-day two religions which are directly descended from Judaism, Christianity and Islam. Unlike the parent faith, both claim to be universal, and to make their appeal, not to any one race or people, but to all humanity. Another point of resemblance is to be found in the fact that each has a historic founder, and can date its origin. Each has a Scripture of its own, and each admits (though in different degrees) the validity of the Jewish Bible. Both are strongly monotheistic, and both have retained something of the ethical character of Judaism, though, again, the conditions under which they arose have produced considerable differences of moral standard. Of the two, Christianity is the older by some six centuries, but it will be more convenient to glance at the younger religion first.

Islam, or Muhammadanism, has been described as "a bastard Christianity," but the name is misleading; it would be much nearer the truth to speak of it as a "bastard Judaism." Except in their universalism, Christianity and Islam agree with one another only when they agree with Judaism, and the differences between Judaism and Islam are much slighter than those which appear when we compare Christianity with either of the other two. Muhammad was certainly acquainted with Christianity, though his comments on it suggest either that his knowledge was very imperfect or that the form of Christianity which he met was far from being normal. It may be doubted whether he had read or heard read any considerable portion of the New Testament, though he was familiar with the name of Jesus and some of the narratives of the Gospel story. He

knew of the doctrine of the Incarnation, which, like the
Jew, he strenuously rejected, though, curiously enough,
he accepted the Virgin Birth of Christ.

Muhammad's knowledge of Judaism was rather more
accurate, but again it does not seem that he had first-hand
acquaintance with the literature. He alludes not infrequently to the narratives of the Old Testament, especially
to those which deal with the early days of Israel. Adam,
Abraham, and Moses are familiar personalities to him,
though there is little trace of the influence of the prophetic
religion in the Qur'an. It may be surmised that he was
dependent for his knowledge of Hebrew history on oral
tradition, and that of a type influenced by Rabbinic
Midrash. In general it may be said that, while he knew
more of Judaism than he did of Christianity, it was not
the best features of that religion which most impressed
themselves upon him.

Our knowledge of pre-Islamic Arabia is comparatively
slight, and our information as to its earlier religion comes
to us partly from traditions handed down by Moslem
authorities, and partly from survivals in Islam itself. We
are indebted especially to two scholars, Wellhausen and
Robertson Smith, for investigating the available material.
Thanks to them we can see something of the general type
of religion current in the time and in the country of
Muhammad, and we can realize that it was not very different from that which prevailed farther north in the early
days of Israel. We hear of a number of different gods, each
of whom was attached to a particular spot or to a particular tribe, though numbers of them might be worshipped in Mecca. Sometimes tribes divided their allegiance
between various deities, but it does not seem that any
attempt was made to relate the gods to one another, and
the religion, while passing out of the purely animistic
stage, is a Polydæmonism rather than a Polytheism.

The ancient Arab recognized many sacred places, and

with each was associated a special ritual. Their main features, however, were very similar, and were such as might be found in almost any Semitic community on the nomad or semi-nomad plane. The symbols of deity were usually simple stones, which served both as emblems of the god or goddess, and, in some respects, as altars. Temples hardly existed; the nearest approach to them was the sacred enclosure, which may have been an extensive pasture area, for camels and other animals were regularly consecrated by being set free to wander and to feed in these spaces. There were sacred times and seasons, though this side of Arabian religion is obscure, owing to the general vagueness of the pre-Islamic calendar. One of the most important was a spring festival which corresponded generally in time and character to the Hebrew Passover. This was regarded as a "pilgrimage festival" (ḥaj), and it was observed, as far as we can tell, at many sacred places. The ritual included a solemn procession round the sacred object, and also, possibly, short journeys from one holy place to another in the immediate neighbourhood.

Sacrifice was a regular feature of the religious life, and the victims included not only all the usual domestic animals, but also human beings, generally captives or slaves. The various kinds of sacrifice that are found in Judaism appear here also, except that the share of the victim devoted to the priest plays a much less important part. The whole picture that is formed in our mind closely resembles that of the early religion of Israel, before and immediately after the entry into Canaan. But whereas the growth of Israelite religion into a Monotheism was a slow process carried over five centuries or more, Islam sprang into the world suddenly, and assumed a stereotyped shape to which all later developments in theory conform.

Whilst the main outlines of the life of Muhammad are familiar to everyone, the facts are too important to be passed over altogether. Born of the ruling family of Mecca,

the Quraish, he nevertheless lived in humble circumstances during the earlier years of his life, and following
his occupation as a camel-driver visited a number of
places outside the actual borders of Arabia. He became
subject to visions, and though the messages he received
in this way probably represented to a large extent the
results of his own thinking, yet they convinced him (and
ultimately others) of the divine origin of the truth he had
to reveal. He was for years saved from violence by his
friends, of whom the two most faithful were his uncle and
his wife, but was at last compelled to flee with a few
converts to Medina. There he organized not only his
religion but also a form of state, established a military
power which lived at first on plunder, and eventually grew
strong enough to return to Mecca, take possession of the
city, and make it his religious and political head-quarters.
His death did not check the progress of his followers, and
within a century Islam had spread by violent means over
the whole of western Asia and northern Africa, and had
actually entered Europe across the straits of Gibraltar.

Islam may be described as a Monotheism in which
every other consideration is subordinated to the doctrine
of the omnipotence of God. He stands essentially alone,
and the great crime is to "associate" others with Him.
He is worthy of all praise, because He can do as He pleases
both in the world of nature and in the world of man. All
things and all persons are utterly subject to Him, and He
is depicted as an absolute despot on the oriental model,
yet with a nature which may be merciful and even loving.
But we cannot help feeling that this omnipotence is purely
arbitrary in its operation; God does as He pleases, subject
to no rule and to no law, whether of others or of His own
being. None can control Him, none can criticize, none can
even forecast the lines on which He will act. Not only will
He bestow material success and disaster where He pleases,
but assigns man to eternal bliss or woe with equal freedom.

He has made all laws, whether physical, moral, or spiritual, and, having made them, can administer or override them as He chooses. Man is helpless, for God has ordained his fate, and it is useless for him to struggle against the authority and will of a supreme personal being. There is, therefore, a fatalism underlying Islam, which, however, is not peculiar to that religion, but characterizes all the thinking of the East, appearing in Indian thought as clearly as elsewhere.

Muhammad inherited the eschatology of the later Judaism, with its clear-cut distinction between the fate of the righteous and that of the wicked after death, an eternal heaven and an eternal hell, a catastrophic end to the material universe and a Day of Judgement. The resurrection is purely physical; the body is to rise as it has been buried, and this belief has led to a horror of mutilation of any kind. Heaven and hell are both described in Moslem theology in material terms, and the one is an endless enjoyment of bodily delights, the other an endless endurance of bodily pain. Thus the wicked "shall be cast into scorching fire to be broiled. They shall be given to drink of a boiling fountain. They shall have no food but of dry thorns and thistles, which shall not fatten neither shall they satisfy hunger." Or again, "They who believe not shall have garments of fire fitted unto them. Boiling water shall be poured on their heads, their bowels shall be dissolved thereby and also their skins, and they shall be beaten with maces of iron. So often as they shall endeavour to get out of hell because of the anguish of their torments, they shall be dragged back into the same; and their tormentors shall say unto them, Taste ye the pain of burning." Heaven, Paradise, or "the Garden," on the other hand, is a place where all delights that men have postponed in life shall be enjoyed, luxurious couches, wine, women (of special creation), fruits, and all manner of pleasant food.

It is impossible to avoid the impression that the great aim which the pious Moslem was exhorted to set before himself was the avoidance of hell and the attainment of Paradise. Both are described in sensuous terms, and it is to be noted that the latter contains no mention of any spiritual happiness such as may be derived from a knowledge of the friendship of God. Muhammad did not teach his followers to rejoice in the loving presence of their Creator; his conception of the future life was from first to last couched in crude and materialistic language, though this may in part be due to the character of his audiences. This was probably inevitable, for neither Muhammad himself nor any of those about him had risen to a plane of thought on which the deeper moral and spiritual issues appealed strongly, though neither the language of Islam nor its interpretation of that language is as stereotyped as some students have supposed. Where men have broken loose and have started thinking for themselves, what they have produced is far less a revised Islam than a new religion, bearing much the same relation to its parent stock as Islam itself does to Judaism.

Muhammad, then, set before his people what was, perhaps, the only ideal that the Arab of his day could appreciate, and he was quite clear as to the means whereby it was to be obtained. Corresponding to the omnipotent despotism ascribed to God was the human attitude of complete surrender to His will. This is brought out in the very name given to the religion: Islam means "the manifesting of humility and submission, and outward conforming with the law of God, and the taking upon oneself to do or to say as the Prophet has done or said."[1] "To become a Moslem" is expressed in Arabic by "aslama," a verb of which "Islam" is the verbal noun. "Moslem" is one who accepts the principles involved in the word "Islam," and a common description of a satisfactory convert

[1] Lane, *Arabic Lexicon*, Bk. I, p. 1,413, col. 2.

K

is "he submitted himself ('aslama') and his submission ('Islam') was good." This allowed no room for argument or discussion, except to determine exactly what the will of God was. It is not part of man's duty to reason or to understand; true religion consists in saying, doing, and being what God commands through his acknowledged media, the Prophets, Muhammad and the Qur'an. Sin is, therefore, any uprising of the human mind or spirit against the orders of the Supreme, a neglect of the obligations imposed on man, the doing of acts which are forbidden by Him.

It is commonly said that two classes of obligation are laid on the Moslem. The first of these includes the six articles of faith, the second the five practical duties. In the former the general name Iman (Creed) is given, to the latter the term Din (Religion) is applied, and whilst the details are variously grouped under the second head, the same practical results always accrue.

The six articles of Faith are as follows:

1. *God.* "There is no God but God" is the foundation of all Muhammadan theology. As we have already seen, the conception of God is derived in the main from the Judaism with which Muhammad was acquainted, and stated that He was the Creator of the universe, the Lord of all humanity, the Disposer of all human affairs, and the Master of the Day of Judgement. With all this He bears the title "Compassionate and Merciful," though these attributes in practice suggest what we should call good nature rather than any deep-seated love for humanity. The whole aim of Moslem thinking about God is to insist on His absolute and unconditioned power. He made Nature, therefore He is Lord of it, and can suspend any of its ordinary workings. Hence one of the tests whereby His presence and will are detected is miracle, and everyone who claims to have the divine message and inspiration must prove his validity by working miracles or having them worked at his request. The belief in the absolute control by God of all human life

is made a separate article of faith; so also is the belief in
the Judgement.

Here we can trace clearly the reaction of the age and
circumstances in which Muhammad lived. All about him
were Polytheists, and to him the greatest of all sins was
that which he called "association," i.e. the recognition of
other deities alongside of Allah. He carries this back into
the distant past, and finds that most of the divine judgements described in the Old Testament were originally due
to a breach of this law. Hence he forbade the making and
worship of idols in the strongest possible terms, apparently
finding from experience that it was the thing itself that
was revered, and not the person whom the thing represented. Since different deities were worshipped under
different forms—the story of the golden calf supplied him
with an illustration—it was unlawful to represent either
in painting or in sculpture the shape of any animal, plant,
or thing, lest the picture or the statue should receive the
homage due to God alone.[1] The result has been an extraordinary limitation of Moslem art. Architecture, music,
and poetry alone are properly admitted under the system
of Islam, and decoration must never include an actual
picture. Geometrical designs are permitted, and the
Arabic writing has lent itself, in some of its forms, to the
elaboration of beautiful figures, though the shapes assumed
by the letters and the arrangement of them sometimes
make the text difficult to read. It is true that on one point
Muhammad was compelled to make concessions to a
tradition which was too strong for his principles, and
allow worship to be paid to the famous black stone at
Mecca known as the Kaaba, but even so Islam remains
the most vigorous protest against idolatry that the world
has ever seen.

[1] Professor A. J. Wensinck, of Leiden, has shown that this prohibition was partly due to the feeling that to make the form of any
creature was, in a sense, to usurp the functions of the Creator.

**2.** *Angels* stand next to God in the order of being. Here, too, Muhammad seems to have been indebted to some extent to Jewish theology, and he even adopted one or two of the names given to Angels in the later Judaism. The term used for them is the Hebrew word meaning "messenger," and their function is to be sent abroad on whatever errands their Lord may have for them. It is curious to note that this doctrine implies (though perhaps unconsciously) a limitation of God. He is unable to be in every place at once, or to be aware of all events at the same moment, or to act universally, and therefore has to employ subordinate spirits. There is also, apparently, the feeling that God is too great to deal with man directly, and that just as a human despot will enforce his will through multitudes of servants, so God Himself has those about Him to whom he can give orders with the certainty that they will be obeyed. Even the great act of revelation, the Qur'an, is mediated to Muhammad through the angel Gabriel.

Below the angels, though more powerful than man, stand the Jinns. These are not strictly included in the article of faith, but they were generally accepted in Muhammad's day and have remained in Islamic thinking as a relic of the old Arabian paganism. Jinns are unlike angels in that they are mortal, and, though created of fire (unlike men) yet they beget children, eat and drink, and take various physical pleasures as human beings do.

**3.** *The Qur'an* is the final revelation of God in literature. Other scriptures are recognized, especially those of the Jew and the Christian, but they are imperfect and temporary. The modern Moslem constantly accuses the Christian of tampering with the Gospel in order to confuse and mislead men, leaving out passages which foretell the coming of Muhammad and insetting others that teach doctrines which Muhammad rejected. On the other hand the Qur'an is as it has existed from all eternity and was revealed to Muhammad. It is the final and infallible

court of appeal for all Moslems, and there is no department
of life over which it is not supreme. This is illustrated by
the familiar story of the destruction of the great library at
Alexandria, on the ground that if the things written in the
books there agreed with the Qur'an they were unnecessary,
if they differed from it they were false. Of course it has
been found that in detail the Qur'an needs supplementing,
and there has grown up a great body of traditions, forming
almost a secondary scripture, but any supplement must
be exegesis, the development of what is already latent in
the Book.

4. *Prophets*. Whilst he claimed to be the medium
through whom the final revelation of God came to men,
Muhammad did not deny the inspiration and truth of his
predecessors. He was the last of a long series of prophets,
and from some points of view claimed to be the restorer of
an ancient religion rather than the founder of a new one.
Six greater prophets are mentioned, of whom Muhammad
is the last, the other five being Adam, Noah, Abraham,
Moses, and Jesus. The dependence on Christianity and
Judaism will be at once recognized, and it is admitted
that each of the other five had his own message to the
world. Abraham is possibly the greatest of them, and
Muhammad claimed that his faith was that of Abraham,
which had been distorted by later generations. But he
himself is more than a Prophet, he is also an Apostle, and
after him no Prophet can enter the world. Divine revelation finds in him its crown and coping-stone.

5. *The Day of Judgement* is also a direct inheritance of
the later Judaism. It is ushered in with the usual apocalyptic signs; the heavens burst asunder, the moon is split,
the sun is folded up, the stars fall, the mountains pass
away. All men and women who have died recover their
bodies, and stand before the throne of the Judge. Conceal-
ment is impossible, for men know their deeds, and God
knows them. The passing of the nations before the Throne

may take years, and to each as he passes is given a "book." Some have it placed in their right hands and find it a passport to Paradise, whilst others have it placed in the left, when it is a writ of condemnation to Hell. The basis on which the decision is passed is the double one, whether they have held the faith of Islam and whether they have performed the acts required of the believer. It follows from the theory of the Prophets and of the old religion (Islam is said to have been the only religion in the world till the death of Abel) that there may have been myriads of good Moslems before Islam, but after Muhammad only those can be admitted to Paradise who have been professed followers of the Apostle.

6. *Predestination.* The doctrine of the absolute omnipotence of God seems always to carry with it the feeling that all events and conduct are ordained by Him. On the other hand, such a doctrine throws the responsibility for moral evil upon God Himself, and relieves men of the ultimate guilt of sin; it is, therefore, seldom carried out to its logical extreme. The paradox is left unsolved, unless it be solved by the doctrine that though man's good works are predestined, God gives him power to acquire them. It is true that men are held responsible for their conduct, and are exhorted to carry out the will of God in terms which have no meaning except when addressed to people of free will, but the formal utterances, where they touch the question, insist on the determination of every human life in all its details. A passage often quoted speaks of the night of "al-Kadr," i.e. "the Decree" or the 27th of Ramadan, as that in which "Angels descend, and the Spirit (Gabriel) also, with the Decree of their Lord on every matter." So also "Thus doth God mislead whom He will and direct aright whom He will," and other passages in the Qur'an enunciate the same doctrine.

Though the practical duties of Islam show some dependence on Jewish law and thought, the influence of the older religion on the younger is not so great as it is in the obligatory doctrines, and it is to be noted that only one of them necessarily affects man's dealings with his neighbour. These are:

1. *Recitation of the Confession of Faith.* This is, as a matter of fact, not enjoined in the Qur'an, but is quite in accordance with the spirit and teaching of Muhammad. The forumla is, of course, the well-known "There is no God but Allah, and Muhammad is His Apostle." No special circumstances are laid down in which it is to be repeated, but it is always used in worship. In theory a Moslem starts every undertaking with the shorter form "In the name of God the compassionate and the merciful."

2. *Prayer.* Whilst private and "unofficial" intercourse with God is not excluded, the object of "official" prayer is not, in Islam, to attain to communion with God, but to satisfy Him by an act of devotion. There are set formulæ, such as "Give me, O Lord, a good entry (into the tomb) and a good exit (from the tomb), and grant me helping power from thy presence." These formulæ are recited in Arabic, even where that language is not understood, and the rite is apt to be tinged with ideas which properly belong to magic. Prayer is enjoined five times a day in the Qur'an, at daybreak (though in one passage, at least, it is possibly the reading of the Qur'an that is intended rather than prayer at this hour), at noon, before sunset, after sunset, and at night. The last period especially is valuable, and the pious Moslem is exhorted to spend half the night in prayer. The words should be said standing or sitting or lying down, with the face turned towards Mecca, and later theory held that it was more meritorious if said in a Mosque. It is interesting to find in the Qur'an special regulations for the prayers of soldiers on active service.

3. *Fasting.* This is prescribed for the month Ramadan. It is obvious that complete abstention from all forms of nourishment and refreshment is impossible for such a

period, and the fast is a fast by day, food and other
necessaries and luxuries being taken after sunset. The
strict Moslem to this day observes it scrupulously, and
abstains from food, water, tobacco, and the like throughout the whole period of daylight. One good meal after
sunset and another before sunrise are usually taken, and
probably the actual quantity of nourishment received
during the twenty-four hours is little less than usual.
Nevertheless, the Fast is sometimes a severe ordeal, for
the Moslem year contains only twelve lunar months of
twenty-nine days, and therefore the months gradually
change their position in the solar year. In a hot country
—and Islam is essentially a religion of hot countries—to
go without water for a whole day in the hottest part of
the year is a serious matter, and the fast still takes its
yearly toll of the weak and the aged.

4. *Alms.* The very high value placed on acts of casual
charity may be an inheritance from Rabbinic Judaism,
where it goes far to take the place of sacrifice. It must be
remembered that there is in the East no organized maintenance for the very poor and helpless, and though the
system is doubtless open to abuse, it has an important
place in daily life.

5. *Pilgrimage.* In theory every Moslem ought, once at
least in his life, to make the pilgrimage to Mecca and
perform the ancient ceremonies, as Muhammad had
himself performed them. These include the compassing of
the Kaaba and the offering of sacrifice, more efficacious
at some times of the year than at others. In actual practice
only a small proportion of the Moslem world can make the
pilgrimage in person, in spite of the greatly increased
facilities provided by modern means of transport. In some
parts of the Moslem world, e.g. in India, it is no uncommon
thing for a village to select one of its inhabitants to go on
pilgrimage, and for his family and neighbours to contribute
jointly to the expense. In this way all share in the per-

VIII]          ISLAM          141

formance of the duty, and all reap some reward in the
accumulation of merit.

These are the five primary duties which are enjoined on
the Moslem. There are others which, if not so binding in
theory, are observed with quite as much regularity and
earnestness. Prominent amongst these is Sacrifice. The
attitude of the Qur'an on this subject is uncertain, and it
may be that Muhammad intended the slaughter of every
animal used for food to have a sacrificial character.
Certainly elaborate directions are given as to the way in
which animals are to be killed, having had the name of
God pronounced over them; the passage in which they
occur suggests that the animal is thus given to God and
then by Him returned to the worshipper for his own use.
But it is clear also that the Mecca ceremonies included the
offering of animals, though these do not seem to have been
burnt, and the modern Islamic world certainly performs
a solemn sacrifice at least once a year. This is at a festival
known as the Bakr 'īd, the "Ox Festival," and it is certainly believed that the sacrifice then performed is
efficacious as an atonement for sin. The normal victim in
India is a cow—a choice possibly due in part to the desire
to protest against Hinduism, and occasionally resulting in
a riot—and in other parts of the Moslem world the victim
is commonly a goat. But there is no ground for the belief,
held in certain quarters, that there is no sacrifice at all in
Islam.

In addition to the positive duties already mentioned,
there are certain prohibitions which should be observed
by all Moslems. These vary in the strength of their urgency,
and some are easily avoided by special dispensation, or
disregarded altogether by some Moslems. There is a list of
forbidden foods and liquors; pork is very generally
abhorred, and wine and all intoxicants are forbidden,
though it is said that in some parts of the world this
command is frequently violated by men who can afford it.

Games of chance are not tolerated, and limitations are placed on music and dancing.

Two other features of the practical life of Islam should be mentioned. One is the duty of the holy war, or the Jihad, which should be waged on the infidels. There is some dispute as to whether this means an offensive war of conquest, whose aim is to subdue or destroy the unbeliever, or a defensive war, which may be necessary to preserve the faith. In any case it seems that it is no longer a practical element in Islam, though from time to time a special vow is taken by a Moslem fanatic to destroy at least one unbeliever before he dies.

The second point which cannot be passed over is the marriage law. Muhammad, as is well known, had a fairly large harem, and found it necessary to justify the later additions by special revelations which applied to himself alone. The law allowed four free wives, but placed no limit on the number of concubines, i.e. slaves, which a man might purchase for himself. The passage in which the rule occurs suggests that it was based on economic as well as on moral considerations, and, as a matter of fact, in many Moslem communities monogamy is the rule. The degrees of kindred affinity within which marriage is forbidden are very similar to those laid down by Jewish and Christian practice. The veiling of women is strictly enjoined, though there is some uncertainty as to the exact meaning of the law in which it is stated, and the actual practice varies a good deal. Women have certain rights in law, and Muhammad was careful to protect their interests and, to some extent, their control over their dowries and other property. But man is declared to be the superior, and retains the right of divorce. This is a very simple proceeding; all that is necessary is that a man should pronounce the formula of dismissal three times. He is not bound to give any reason for his conduct, and the wife's right of divorce is limited. In general it may be said that while the original standard

of marriage was never so high as that which has normally
prevailed amongst Christians and Jews (and it is possible
that the standard was meant to be higher than the actual
practice sometimes is), it was probably an improvement
on conditions which were normal amongst the heathen
Arabs of Muhammad's own time.

In general it may be said that Muhammad recognized
the *Lex Talionis* as the basis of civil and criminal law,
though again he probably did much to mitigate the
severity of existing custom, particularly by permitting a
money composition in cases of murder and of some other
offences.

We may, then, sum up the main features of the religion
of Muhammad as depicted in the Qur'an. It represented
God as an absolute, omnipotent, somewhat capricious, but
benevolent despot. He made Himself known to man by
three channels, by prophets, occasionally by angels, and,
for the great mass of men, by the Qur'an. Man might draw
near to him by worship, fasting, pilgrimage, and sacrifice,
but the practical ideal of the religion was not so much
fellowship with God as the attainment of a sensuous
Paradise after death. Sin might be either theological
heresy or immoral practice, though the ethical standard is
noticeably lower than in Buddhism, Confucianism, or
Judaism. Atonement might be impossible; it rested on the
will of God, though much might be done to influence Him
through righteous living and through sacrifice.

Though Islam has changed less in the course of its
history than any other religion, there have been differences
of opinion and additions made to the original form of the
faith. There are, for instance, four schools, each traced
back to an historic founder, all of which are reckoned as
equally orthodox, and each is represented in the great
Moslem University of Cairo. On the other hand, there
are numerous sects which refuse to recognize one another,
and are inclined to class their rivals with the unbelievers.

The two best known of these great sects are those called the Sunni and the Shiah. The differences between them are historical rather than doctrinal, and each regards the other as schismatic rather than heretical, for both can lay equal claim to strict observance of the Qur'an and of all other religious duties, except that the Shiah is practically excluded from Mecca and makes his pilgrimage to the shrine of a saint of his own sect. The quarrel between the two goes back to the earliest days of Islam. On the death of Muhammad he was succeeded in the leadership of the Faithful by Abu Bekr, Omar, and Othman, all of whom had been companions of the Prophet. Othman had married two of his daughters, but none of the three was strictly of Muhammad's blood. The fourth Caliph, however, was Ali, descended from Muhammad through his daughter Fatima. He was assassinated after a reign of six years, and was succeeded by his son Hasan. The latter gave place to a certain Muavia, the founder of the Omeyid dynasty, and was eventually murdered. His only brother, Hosein, made an attempt to secure the Caliphate, after the death of Muavia, but was attacked and slain on his way from Mecca to Mesopotamia, leaving the Omeyids in possession.

The Shiahs insist that the Caliphate was intended to be hereditary, and that the first legitimate successor of Muhammad was Ali. To them the murders of Hasan and Hosein rank as the most terrible crimes in history; the memory of the two brothers is kept alive at the festival of the Moharram, and the tomb of Hosein at Kerbela ranks second only to Mecca as a place of pilgrimage to the Shiah. It should be remarked that the Moharram is observed by all Moslems, but whilst it is an occasion of joy for Sunnis, for Shiahs it is a time of bitter mourning. In parts of the world where, as in India, Sunnis and Shiahs are both found in fairly equal numbers, the Moharram is often an occasion of fierce conflict between the two sects. Generally speaking, however, the Shiahs predominate in Persia, and are numerous in India; the rest of the Moslem world is mainly, though not exclusively, Sunni.

Other sects have appeared from time to time, which had differed a good deal more from orthodox Islam than did Sunni and Shiah from one another. Among these, the Wahhabis, were a vigorous reforming sect, the Puritans of Islam. They aimed at, and for a time secured, a large extent of political power, and in recent years they have overrun all central and western Arabia. Their original protest was aimed at the worship of the saints, and even adoration paid to Muhammad was condemned.

Amongst the Shiahs there has arisen one very important movement. The theory that the descendants of Ali were the only rightful Caliphs still persists, and a list of eleven of them is recorded. Of these the last is still living, though he is concealed, and waiting to be revealed to the world when the time is ripe for him. From time to time men have arisen who have claimed to be either this twelfth *Imam* (whose name is *Mahdi*) or to be in close touch with him. The movement has had a serious political aspect in northern Africa, and the theory serves as a useful excuse for turbulent and revolutionary spirits.

In two directions Mahdism has given birth to forms of doctrine which seem rather to claim to be new religions than to be sects of Islam. One of these, arising in Persia, is Bahaism, which has attracted a good deal of attention in recent years. It has been driven out of Persia, but still survives in Syria, though it has suffered so much from internal dissensions, that it seems to be already a spent force. The other took its rise in India, and claimed to be a fulfilment of the expectations of Islam, Christianity, and Hinduism. Like Bahaism, it professes to be universal, though it still retains formally the name of Islam. In so far as either has tried to reform Islam, it seems that both have failed, for neither has made great headway amongst Moslems. On the other hand, both have achieved a certain success in making converts from the non-Moslem world, and may, in this and in other respects, be compared with an eclectic movement like that which is usually called Theosophy.

It is impossible rightly to represent Islam without some reference to Sufism. The Sufis are sometimes spoken of as if they were a separate sect, and it is often assumed that they are more or less heterodox. But they generally regard themselves as orthodox, and representatives are to be found in all branches of Islam, though they are probably most numerous amongst the Persian Shiahs. Their existence illustrates an outstanding weakness of the religion of the Qur'an, which leaves comparatively little room for the development of mysticism, though, of course, the language of Scripture, in Islam as elsewhere, can usually be interpreted in any sense that may be desired. Sufism may be due largely to the influence of other religions, both in its theory and in its practice, but it may safely be said that such influence would have had little effect unless it met a deep-seated need for which primitive Islam made no provision.

Sufism seems to have originated as an ascetic movement. There is, of course, no place in the scheme of Muhammad for monastic orders, such as those which appear both in Buddhism and in some forms of Christianity. Nevertheless, there is a special appeal which is made by the austerities and sacrifices of the professed life, and there soon arose within Islam men who copied the Christian hermits in their dress and practices. From the coarse woollen garment (Arabic, *suf*) which they wore, they received the name Sufi. Their theology was quite orthodox, but laid particular stress on the doctrine of God's absolute authority, and on the corresponding demand for complete human submission to His will.

From this point it seems that Sufism advanced to a mysticism like that which is so often found in Christianity, and appears also both in some forms of Vaishnava Hinduism and of Amitabha Buddhism. The Sufi concentrated on

the love of God, and poured out his spirit in communion
with Him. His language was often extravagant, and in its
attempt to depict heavenly things in earthly terms gave
rise to frequent misunderstanding. But a Christian who is
familiar with Charles Wesley's "Jesu, Lover of my soul,"
or with Augustine's "When wilt thou intoxicate me?"
ought not to mistake the real meaning of figures of speech
which, if taken literally, might suggest devotion to women
and to wine. There can be no doubt of the genuineness of
the Sufi's experience of God.

Sufi theology developed along lines which we may not
unjustly call pantheistic. The sense of intimate communion with God led to the thought of absolute identity
with Him. It may be that the Sufis were influenced by
Hindu or Buddhist philosophy, but it is equally possible
that their beliefs on this head grew up spontaneously from
their experience. Yet they were still able to maintain the
forms of orthodoxy, for they could repeat the test creed
"There is no God but Allah," though they interpreted it
in a new sense. To them it became practically what the
Vedanta thinker meant by his confession of faith "ONE
exists without a second." They saw God in the universe
and in man, and therefore claimed themselves to be
inseparable and, indeed, indistinguishable from Him.

Thus the mystic sense of communion with a person gave
place, as an ideal, to the loss of independent consciousness,
and the Sufi adopted measures which might induce an
ecstatic state like that of the old Canaanite prophet. A
special class named Dervishes gave themselves especially
to exercises which should induce this ecstasy, and their
wild dance has become a characteristic feature of some
forms of Moslem sainthood. At the same time there is
reason to fear that the ethical sense has weakened, and
Sufism affords one more illustration of the tendencies
which seem inevitable when once the stress on personality
as the basis of religion has been lost.

## IX.—CHRISTIANITY

In Islam we have a descendant of Judaism which was influenced rather by its legal and Rabbinic features; in Christianity we have a faith which owes more to the teaching of the Hebrew prophets, and, perhaps, in its earlier and more elementary forms, to popular Jewish Apocalyptic. Muhammad's interest in the religion of the Old Testament is at its height in the story of Abraham, and almost ceases after Moses; whilst it would not be true to say that the Christian is not concerned with anything before Moses (e.g. some forms of Christian theology lay great stress on the accounts of the Creation and of the Fall), there can be no doubt that for the Christian the centre of importance lies in such men as Isaiah and Jeremiah. Further, many early Christian thinkers were undoubtedly influenced by Greek philosophy, though they may have known it best in its Jewish-Alexandrian, or perhaps Antiochian, garb. Throughout its history Christianity has shown itself capable of a high degree of elasticity in its forms of expression, and has from time to time been ready to restate its fundamental doctrines in terms which, while preserving the essence of its creed, have been adapted to the moving thought of successive generations.

Christianity inherits its doctrine of God from Judaism; it is not an accident that Jesus was a Jew. That is to say, its theology is monotheistic, and the first article of its creed is that there is but one God. Its Jewish ancestry makes it impossible for it to offer a pantheistic explanation of the universe (in the strict sense of the term) without abandoning at once its relationship to its Founder. The whole teaching of Jesus, moral and spiritual, is based on the unexpressed but yet fundamental assumption that God is a Person, who is differentiated from all human persons, as they are from one another, not by some variant essential quality (unless infinity is regarded as a quality and not a degree), but by a separate individuality and identity.

This does not exclude the possibility of identifying Him with that ultimate which is the goal of all metaphysical quest. Christianity can speak of God, not merely as *loving*, but as *Love*; not merely as *true*, but as *Truth*; not merely as *living*, but as *Life*; perhaps not merely as *Creator*, but as *Creativeness*; not merely as *Cause*, but as *Causation*. Nevertheless, Christianity started as a religion with a very strong personal basis, and whilst it leaves room for a metaphysical conception of God, it insists that for practical religion the attribute which is relevant is Personality.

There is, then, one personal God, the Creator of the whole material universe, and the Lord of all that exists. Opinions differ even amongst Christians as to the extent to which that lordship is exercised over men, some (though comparatively few to-day in proportion to the whole number of Christians) holding a fatalistic doctrine, the majority believing that, in creating self-conscious and self-determining beings such as man, He definitely assumes a limitation, seeking to control His human creatures by moral and not by mechanical means, and recognizing to the full their personal status. This appears in the term used for God by the Founder of Christianity, who speaks of Him as Father. The implications of that name may be said to be briefly these. He is the author of all human being, and at the same time assumes a definite moral relationship to men, and, within the limits imposed by the law of personality, responsibility for them. His own character is

L

perfectly good, and men may find in Him, carried to an infinite degree, all those qualities that they recognize as good in their own personality. He is thus perfectly wise, perfectly just, perfectly true, perfectly loving, and will manifest these and all other good qualities in His dealings with His children.

Christian metaphysical theology speaks of three "Persons" within the being of God, Father, Son, and Spirit. The term "Person," however, is misleading, and is due to an unfortunate Latin equivalent of a word used in an ancient Greek creed. The usual formula in English, inherited from the Latin, is "three Persons in one Substance," but, as even medieval theologians of the Latin Church recognized, a more correct rendering of the original words would be "three Substances in one Essence." But it may safely be said that the creeds which enshrine this doctrine are the result of conflicting forces in the thought of the early Church, which sought to guard against two opposite misunderstandings of its view, and produced a formula which probably very few can claim fully to understand. We are on surer ground if we regard the use of three terms, Father, Son, and Spirit, as the result of the actual experience of Christians, who developed them—for they did not invent them; all three were in use in some side or other of Judaism—in order to distinguish different modes of the knowledge of God.

Christianity thinks of the revelation of God as appearing in four ways, the last alone being final and complete. These are:

1. *Nature.* The material world, being created by God, whether creation be evolutionary or catastrophic, must of necessity be in some fashion an expression of His will and being. Traditional "arguments"—reasons why men may find themselves intellectually satisfied as to the existence of God—are based on the facts of the material world. From the repeated chain of cause and effect, the

link which seems to find different events together, men have argued to a "First Cause," not merely in the sense that there is a cause which starts the chain, an event which is followed by all others and preceded by none, but rather in the sense that the existence of the link named cause cannot be an accident, but must in itself be the product of a Mind and Will. Further, the phenomena of order and of adaptation of organ to function in the material universe seem to point to a Mind which can plan the whole, and to a Power which can give effect to the design of the Mind. Yet Christianity never claims that the whole or even the more important features of the character and being of God are revealed in Nature. Jesus Himself seems to have thought of all Nature as being good, at least in the sense of being either beneficial or harmless to spiritual humanity, but it is always admitted that it is only in a minor degree that Nature can be called moral. The final revelation of God to man must be above all things ethical, and the general judgement that will be passed on Nature is that it is non-moral. It may lead the seeker back to a being of great, but possibly limited, intelligence, and of great, but possibly limited, power, but the traces of loving care, though not absent, are less conspicuous:

> "*Is there strength there? Enough: intelligence?*
> *Ample: but goodness in a like degree?*
> *Not to the human eye in the present state,*
> *An isoscele deficient in the base.*"

2. *Inspired men and women.* Christianity recognizes that the Spirit of God (or God the Spirit) may and does enter into men and women, and use them as the means whereby His truth may be made known. The doctrine is difficult to formulate, because it is held in so many different ways. Sometimes the inspiration is thought to be confined to a limited number of men, those whose writings are preserved in the Bible, and perhaps other prophets whose

exact utterances have not been handed down to us. Again, it is sometimes said that wherever a man becomes conscious of a truth, and strives to express it in any way, through literature, art, music, or otherwise, he is inspired, and in this case inspiration is almost synonymous with genius. Others believe that there is something divine— not merely some personal element which resembles God, but an actual portion of the divine essence and being, a "something of God"—in every man, and that this may make him a medium for the communication of the truth and nature of God, though it is stronger in some persons than in others and may be cultivated. In some forms of Christianity, perhaps in all, there prevails a belief that in the assembly or body of Christians—called "the Church" —this same Spirit is always to be found, leading, teaching, and inspiring its members. Whilst Jesus Himself is regarded as the final revelation of God, He still needs exposition, His words need to be studied and reinterpreted, perhaps by every generation, and practically all Christians believe that they have with them the guidance of the Holy Spirit in this task.

Amongst most bodies of Christians this permanent inspiration is especially manifested in a particular class of men, who, in the eyes of many, form "the Church" in a narrower sense. They are men who have been "ordained," and there are a number of "orders" of clerical persons, varying in the degree in which they are repositories of the divine Spirit. Whilst it is not clear that Jesus Himself personally authorized the appointment of such orders, or indicated that a special power attached to them, the theory goes back to a very early stage in its development. Within the New Testament itself there are signs that differences of function were recognized, and a writer living hardly more than a century after the death of Jesus could say that no Church, properly so called, can exist apart from the presence of Deacons, Bishops, and Elders.

It is widely held in the Christian Church that the gift of the Holy Spirit can be, and must be, conferred through some special ritual. For the lay Christian, Baptism is the recognized rite. Originally an actual immersion in water, held to symbolize the burial and resurrection of Jesus, it has amongst many Christians become a pouring of water upon the head, or even the sprinkling of a few drops, and most bodies of Christians administer this rite to infants, in order that any spiritual gift which is conveyed by it may be theirs at the start of life. Most Christian bodies mark by a further special rite the point at which the adolescent or adult enters into full conscious membership of the Church. Similarly in the appointment of clergy of all grades there is usually some ceremonial observed, which includes the laying of the hands of a qualified person on the candidate, the underlying theory stating that by this act a continuous stream of inspiration is preserved and transmitted. Many sacred acts are possible only to persons who have thus been consecrated, and these generally include the pronouncement of absolution on confession, and the administration of "sacraments" (though Baptism may, in case of need, be administered by laymen, and even by women).

The other Sacraments also are rites through which special communication of divine power and nature are made to men—"outward and visible signs of an inward and spiritual grace." The number of rites thus recognized varies in different sections of the Christian Church, but Baptism and the Eucharist (or Lord's Supper) are always included amongst them, and also, generally, Marriage. But there are wide differences of interpretation and practice in the Sacraments, some regarding them as means whereby God is enabled to enter into human life in a special sense, others thinking of them as purely human acts of worship which have a solemnity and an efficacy greater than those of the ordinary methods. But it should be remarked that there are bodies of Christians—notably the "Society of Friends"—who insist that no material ceremony or external ritual can be held to be in itself a means of the communication of the Holy Spirit, and that God always works by direct contact with the human soul.

3. *Scripture.* All Christians accept the Bible as the Word of God, though there are differences of opinion both as to the actual extent of the Bible and as to the way in which its inspiration is to be regarded. Some sections of the Church include in their Old Testament only the old Jewish Hebrew (and Aramaic) Canon, some add other books included in the Greek Old Testament but not in the Hebrew Bible. These are sometimes grouped by themselves (where they are not recognized as fully canonical) under the title of the "Apocrypha" or the "Deuterocanonical" books. The New Testament is practically always the same, except that some eastern Christians regard the Apocalypse and four of the shorter Epistles as being on a lower level of canonicity.

The degree of inspiration ascribed to Scripture also varies. Some Christians hold a view which is almost comparable to the Moslem theory of the Qur'an, believing that every word in its pages must be accepted as literally the inspired word of God, and that there must be no discussion either as to date, authorship, historicity of events described in it, or apparent discrepancies and contradictions. It is psychologically a curious fact that Christians who hold this view generally rely for the authentic text, not on the Hebrew or Greek original, but on the standard text of a translation. Others take the view that the writers are inspired rather than the written word, and that allowance has to be made for the human medium through which the message has been transmitted. But practically all Christians recognize that in the Bible we have a revelation of God of a different kind from that which we have in any other literature.

4. *Incarnation.* This is the central, and indeed the final, mode of revelation, and though it is expressed in many different ways, yet all Christians agree that "God was in Christ, reconciling the world unto Himself." Again there are wide differences in the way in which the Incarnation is described. In this connection the doctrine of the Virgin Birth should be mentioned, which makes Christ human through His mother, though He had no material Father. This avoids the taint of hereditary guilt, which one theory of the origin of sin attaches to all humanity, and also meets the feeling, especially common in the ancient world, that there is something positively sinful in the ordinary means of propagation. There is, however, in some quarters a feeling that this form of the doctrine offers an incomplete Incarnation, and that it is preferable to think of Him as being born in the normal way. There are many ways in which the combination of the human and the divine is described, an attempt being made to differentiate between the two elements in His consciousness or nature. Sometimes the divine is said to pervade His whole nature, sometimes it is concentrated in the will, sometimes relegated to the unconscious. A modern tendency is to regard Him as psychologically human, with no consciousness of His own Deity, in the belief that only so can the Incarnation be a complete and perfect fact. But, however it may be described, the Incarnation is a doctrine held by all Christians, who believe that "the Word became flesh and dwelt amongst us."

Four accounts of the life of Jesus are recognized as "canonical." Of these four, three present a common picture, and are therefore sometimes called the "Synoptic Gospels," while the fourth, though not to be set on one side as "unhistorical," presents rather the Christ of the mystical experience. The main facts accepted by all Christians and attested by all four of these documents (which are generally supposed to date, in their present

form, from thirty to seventy years after the death of
Jesus) are as follows. Jesus was a Jewish peasant whose
home was in the Galilean village of Nazareth. His active
ministry was limited to a period not exceeding three years,
during which He lived the life of a wandering teacher. He
met with the hostility of official Judaism early in His
public work, and thereafter confined His direct teaching
to a small band of chosen followers. Finally, having
secured their personal allegiance, He deliberately made His
way to Jerusalem, in order to complete His life-work there
by being crucified. He was executed by Pontius Pilate, the
Roman Procurator of Judea, on a charge of treason against
the Empire, brought by the official heads of the Jewish
people. His death and burial are circumstantially described, and it is stated that on the third day after His
execution He was seen to be alive by His followers, who,
inspired by His resurrection, began within a few weeks to
proclaim Him as the Messiah, shortly to return and end
the age. A fifth historical document, known as the "Acts
of the Apostles," together with a number of letters written
by members of the early Church, amongst whom Paul of
Tarsus is the most conspicuous, show how the community
of His followers grew from a small Jerusalem sect into a
Church whose limits would in the end be those only of the
human race.

No other religion attaches such importance to its
historical founder as does Christianity, though the
Christian position is approached by some forms of Mahayana Buddhism. Jesus is to the Christian not only the
world's final religious and moral teacher; He is at once the
supreme revelation of God and the most certain avenue to
God. One of the most significant sayings attributed to Him
is "I am the way, the truth, and the life." Many Christians
in practice identify Him completely with God, and pray,
not merely *through* Him but *to* Him, finding that their
experience of communion with God is one of union with

Him. This is true even of so early a convert as Paul, and he has been followed by innumerable Christian mystics. From the very first, Christians found in the resurrection of Jesus the seal of His authority and mission, and the pledge of their own eternal life in God. In contact with the grosser life of the non-Jewish world the early Missionaries —again Paul is the best known—saw in the need for a deep and regenerating moral atonement their most urgent problem, and they found full satisfaction in the death of Jesus. More than one explanation was given of the way in which an atonement was thus secured, but the central thought goes back to Jesus Himself, for the best attested saying we have from Him connected His own death with the consummation of the spiritual history, at least of Israel.

From the human side the approach to God is made in two ways. One is by the exercise of faith, a word which has a great many different meanings applied to it. In some quarters it is assumed to consist in theological orthodoxy, but it can hardly be maintained that this sense is original, and nearly all Christians would insist that something further is needed. Perhaps the most generally acceptable description of faith would be one which stated that it involves a direct personal relation between God and the individual soul. Christianity always has a mystical element, and there can be no true faith where there is no mysticism, though it will vary considerably with different temperaments. One element in faith is always a belief in the spiritual world and the grasp of it through (and perhaps in spite of) the material. It is, in part, a conviction that "the things that are seen are temporary, but the things that are not seen are eternal." But it is more than this. It involves of necessity a surrender, a casting of the individual spirit on God, an acceptance of Him as the Father, an entrusting to Him of the whole of the self. This may be expressed in even stronger terms, and some

Christians can speak of "dying with Christ," "living no longer, except in so far as they live in Christ," "abiding in Christ," and there are other phrases which imply that faith means a moral unification of the human with the divine.

In many forms of Christianity (and perhaps theoretically in all) there is a doctrine of conversion. This varies with different views of human nature. Some theologians insist (though the view is less common than it used to be) that man is hereditarily evil, not merely in the sense of possessing tendencies which are likely to lead him away from God, but in being tainted with ancestral guilt and being therefore naturally sinful. It is clear that such a theory requires that there should be a definite point in the history of the individual at which the passage is made from the old sinful state into the state of faith. Even where a doctrine of original sin is not held, many persons find themselves in a condition which they recognize as being apart from and away from God, and feel that they need to take a definite step which shall bring them into harmony with the divine life. And probably in the life of all Christians there is a time when they either become conscious of God for the first time, or realize that a stage in their spiritual development has been reached, though the actual process of entering the life of faith has been slow and possibly imperceptible. Most Christian bodies mark such a point in development or change by some definite ritual, though the theory varies, some holding that the ritual is an expression of an experience, others believing that it confers it.

The second principal means of the approach of the soul to God is to be found in worship. Faith is a permanent attitude and habit of spirit, and forms the background, or, to use another metaphor, the atmosphere, of the Christian's life. But, in the nature of the case, it cannot always occupy the surface of the mind, nor receive conscious attention. At the same time such a definite turning of the self to God is necessary, and indeed inevitable, if the true state of faith exists. It is in this that worship consists, whether it be that of the individual or that of a larger body, congregation or Church. Prayer, which is the centre of worship, is always properly the effort of the human spirit to enter into direct contact with the divine. It is the upward movement of man to God, the attempt to enter into direct communion. It has many modes of expression. Many Christians find value in the use of set forms of words which, originally expressing the experience of others, seem to apply to and describe their own needs and state. Sometimes a special virtue is supposed to inhere in the words themselves, and there is in certain cases even a tendency for the formulæ to become almost magical, especially where the ecclesiastical language is not the vernacular, and is understood badly, if at all, by the worshipper. Yet even so it is probably true that the conscious turning of the heart and thought to God has its effect and helps to win the sense of communion. Often it is supposed that prayer is mainly petition, a series of requests offered by the children to their Father for things which they or others need, though it is not often that the Christian allows his conception of prayer to fall so low as to think of it as a means whereby man can impose his will on God.

The later Judaism and Islam developed a public worship, in which a body of persons, by uniting with one another in prayer and other exercises, sought to attain a more complete effect than could be produced by the worship of isolated units. Such worship is also characteristic of all forms of Christianity. Based on a saying of Jesus, "Where two or three are gathered together in my name, there am I in the midst of them," it forms one of the recognized means of the human approach to God. Experience has shown that the spiritual power of a united body of persons is more effective as a rule than isolated action, and though, doubtless, there is the danger that it may degenerate into a kind of magical formalism or a means of more or less sensuous enjoyment, there can be no question either of its general value or of its practical necessity for the maintenance of the life of faith.

Methods of worship vary greatly, but in nearly all bodies of Christians the central act is a ritual which is connected with the death of Jesus. Both the form of the ritual and the theory of it vary amongst different bodies of Christians, but it is always traced back to the last meal which Jesus shared with His disciples before His crucifixion, and the two elements of bread and wine are always present. The former represents, suggests, or recalls the body of Christ, the latter His blood, in accordance with His own words at that meal.

Four main types of theory may be distinguished. The first is that to which the name "transubstantiation" is given. This doctrine is based on a distinction between the "form" and the "substance," and states that after certain words during the service have been pronounced over the elements, they become "in substance" the very Body and Blood of Christ. They preserve the form—that is, all the physical appearance—of bread and wine, but in reality they have undergone a change, and the recipient does in truth partake of the very essence of Christ. Somewhat similar is the view known as "consubstantiation," according to which the words of consecration introduce a new substance, of supreme spiritual value, alongside of the material substance which previously existed alone. This theory is characteristic of the Lutheran branch of the Protestant Church, and is historically due to the difficulty which Luther himself and his followers felt in interpreting the words of Christ, "this is my body," in a metaphorical sense. A third type of theory may be described as "receptionist," where a distinction is made amongst those who actually partake of the elements. To those who

rightly discern the divine presence and are spiritually fit
to receive it, the bread and the wine are the very Body
and Blood of Christ; to others they remain simply the
material substances which they were before being consecrated. In the fourth place the whole ritual is regarded
as a simple but very solemn memorial, whose aim is to
remind the participants, in a peculiarly impressive way,
of the death of Christ, and of what that death means to
them. It may be added (though this view is not officially
maintained by any of the great Christian sects) that there
are those who hold that the words of institution were not
intended to inaugurate any special ritual, but applied to
every meal in which Christians shared. Whenever Christians ate and drank together, they were to use the occasion
to remind them of the death of Christ.

It follows from what has been said of the nature and
being of God that the Christian ideal is a personal relationship between God and man. The insistence on personality
as the final form of reality for religion, inherited from
Judaism, makes it inevitable that the highest aim that
can be set before a Christian is personal. Now the greatest
experience that a person can know is that of friendship,
varying in degrees, but finding its culmination in something for which even love seems too narrow and too weak
a term. It is a sense of moral unity, in which both parties
retain their individuality, and yet recognize that they
are as one, linked together by the love, trust, knowledge
that exists between them. It implies a complete surrender
of the whole of the self, with all feelings, capacities, and
powers, and can only be truly fulfilled when that surrender
is mutual. It appears in the higher forms of friendship even
between two human persons, though there it can never be
perfect because neither of the individuals is perfect, but
it approaches the ideal in proportion as both parties attain
to self-abnegation in their relation one to another. In
human experience it can reach its acme only in friendship

with God, and Christianity offers to man a God who gives
Himself utterly and without stint or reservation (save
such as may be imposed by the law of His own consistency)
to man, and seeks to win from man a like consecration.
Avoiding the sexual suggestion which sometimes creeps
into the connotation of such terms as love (though the
Christian mind does not see anything necessarily wrong in
sex), Jesus spoke of God as Father, and assumed that the
perfect relationship could be compared to that which
would exist in an ideal family life between the parent and
the child. Jesus is, in religious experience as in all else, the
perfect model which the Christian aims at following, and
to Him God was not only the most real fact of all experience, but the closest and most intimate of all possible or
conceivable friends. Nothing is more characteristic of Him
than this unique sense of God as one whom He knew so
well as to make a breach or a misunderstanding utterly
impossible, and He has imported into the term "Father"
a meaning which has immeasurably exalted the noblest
and purest of human relations. Many of His followers, too,
have found their sense of this friendship concentrated in
personal love and loyalty to Jesus Himself.

From this ideal springs the Christian conception of
immortality. No doubt in the minds of many Christians
the thought of Heaven is complicated by ideas which have
survived from Judaism and perhaps other religions, but
in no case can a Christian think of Heaven apart from God.
Jesus enlarged and simplified the moral argument for a
continued life after death which had developed in Pharisaic
Judaism by insisting that a personal relation with an
eternal God must be as enduring as that God Himself.
A physical accident like death—for Jesus also spiritualized
the conception—could never finally sever the intimacy
between two personal beings, one of whom was admittedly
eternal by nature. From the first, too, Christians have
found their belief in a future life strengthened by, and

sometimes based on, the Resurrection of Jesus Himself. The Christian view of immortality is in some ways nearer to the Greek than to the Hebrew, for it is essentially an extension of spiritual life beyond the grave, but it is none the less the real descendant of the teaching of the Old Testament Prophets on the character of God.

It goes without saying that the Christian ideal is not easy of attainment, and even when reached consciously is liable to be lost temporarily. No religion, not even Judaism at its best, has a keener sense of sin. And, from the stress laid on the moral character of God, it follows that the Christian view of sin is always moral. It is not necessarily confined to acts which violate the highest laws of human conduct, though it goes without saying that a real offence against man is also an offence against God. The matter goes deeper, and sin is not merely an act or a habit, it is an attitude of soul. It may be compared to a disease of which wrong deeds are merely symptoms, and the trouble cannot be cured simply by external treatment. Christian thinkers constantly repeat that upright conduct alone can never wipe out the effects of sin past and gone, and that the requirements of God can never be wholly met by mere morality. Sin is in its essence a wrong attitude to God, and such an attitude is certain to exhibit itself in conduct.

Sin is its own punishment. It is true that other sanctions have from time to time been recognized, but it is still not certain that any other was intended in the earliest forms of Christian teaching. The language of Jewish (and perhaps Greek) eschatology was freely used to describe the Hell which is reserved for impenitent sinners, but it is quite possible that this should be taken as metaphor describing —and, be it noted, quite inadequately—an existence after death apart from God. It is interesting to observe how little stress a thinker like Paul lays on the avoidance of Hell. There are also hints of a possible doctrine of "conditional immortality," which would teach that the soul dies with the body unless it is in real harmony and communion with God. A third view, widely held amongst Christians, states that all sin must be purged away with suffering of some kind, and that although this can be met to some extent by confession and voluntary suffering during life on earth, yet it can only be completed after death in a Purgatory, whence the purified spirit may at last pass into Heaven. But whatever sanction may be applied before or after death, it is laid down by Christian teaching from the first that sin produces its effect upon the sinner. In a certain sense Christianity holds as strictly to a law of Karma as do Hinduism and Buddhism, though the doctrine is not carried to the same absolute conclusion. "Whatsoever a man soweth, that shall he also reap" is the early statement of the truth, and whatever escape from the consequences of sin may be offered by the Christian Atonement, it does not include the freeing of the sinner himself (and others) from the natural results of his wrongdoing.

It is in the Atonement that Christianity differs from all other religions, perhaps because the need for a moral reunion is so much the greater owing to the heavier stress on sin. All Christians agree that it is in the death of Jesus, in whom is to be seen the incarnate God, that the practical problem of reconciliation is solved. It is not an accident that the symbol of Christianity is the Cross, for there lies its *differentia* and its centre. There are two dangers which beset every religion in presenting its atonement to its adherents. The first is the difficulty which arises when the atonement is made from the human side. There are, no doubt, old beliefs, almost superstitions, which teach the effect of various modes by which atonement is made. As we have already seen, the religious ideal is attained in some forms of faith by prayer, and this may even be held to have so magical an effect on the deity to whom it is offered that he cannot withhold his favour. In some, religious knowledge, or the admission and acceptance of truth, appears to be sufficient—some forms of Buddhist and Hindu doctrine will serve as illustrations. But most often the atonement is safely secured only by some act of sacrifice, and the rites enjoined from time to time suggest that there is not merely an offering made to a god, which will induce him to lay aside his anger and assume a gracious and even generous frame of mind, but that there is some special value in the blood, representing the life, of the victim. Poured partly on the altar and partly on the penitent, it may serve to reunite them in a covenant which is the ideal of the religion, but which has, nevertheless, been broken by some human act or attitude. In all cases the act is performed by or on behalf of the sinner; it is an atonement made from the human side. Yet too often, perhaps always, while it may induce a temporary sense of relief and a partial recovery of that which is sought, it is the general experience that it fails to offer a permanent renewal of the right relationship between the sinner and the deity against whom he has sinned. Even in Judaism some of the noblest spirits were conscious of the weakness and inefficiency of sacrifice, and that when it involved the surrender of the very best that man had to offer. Nor does it seem that such external acts are effective (though there may be something deeper on the part of the worshipper) in producing such a real moral reunion of the human with the divine as Christianity sets before its worshippers. In other words, regarded from the highest standpoint, even sacrifice is a failure, and if sacrifice fails the last effort that can be made by man has been made and has not achieved its final goal. Experience seems to show that no atonement made from the human side can be finally valid.

On the other hand we have the danger that even where atonement is made from the divine side, forgiveness being granted for wrongs done, it may be taken too easily and too lightly. The very strongly personal view of God held,

M

for instance, in ancient Israel allowed men to believe that Yahweh was kindly and forgiving, and that His wrath might be easily appeased. The result was inevitably a weakening of the seriousness of sin. In some modern Christian circles a similar phenomenon has manifested itself. An undue stress on the implications of Divine omnipotence, conceived almost in a sense more suitable to Islam than to Christianity, and a corresponding insistence on the consequences of sin to the sinner in the hereafter, have been followed by a revulsion of feeling and a discovery that, after all, God, as Jesus expounded Him, is a Father, and fathers would not persecute their children vindictively to all eternity for minor indiscretions or even for more heinous sins. Sin has therefore been taken lightly and easily: "He's a good fellow, and 'twill all be well," "Of course He will forgive; it is His profession," has been the attitude.

Against both these points of view the Christian doctrine of atonement stands as an emphatic protest. No valid reconciliation can be made from the human side; Christian belief asserts that "God was in Christ, reconciling the world unto Himself." And, as against the light and shallow view of sin and its meaning, it asserts that Christ, in whom it recognizes God incarnate, "Himself bare our sins in His own body on the tree." That is to say the atonement is made from God's side, and it is made in a form which, so far from suggesting that it is a light or easy thing, insists that God only accomplishes it at the cost of infinite pain to Himself. God suffers; that is perhaps the centre of what Christianity has to offer the world. God suffers through His own personal qualities at the hands of those whom He has made and loves. For there can be no love without at least the capacity for suffering, and there can be no suffering at its deepest unless it be inflicted by one who is loved. The Christian doctrine of the atonement has taken many different forms during the history of Christianity. Some of these are obsolete, and others appeal only to small sections of the Christian Church. But all agree, however different in detail the theories may be, that it is the death of Christ which gives to Christianity its supreme message, and here that this religion finds the solution of its great problem. Its universal, indeed its only possible, symbol is a Cross.

Like all other great religions, Christianity is divided into several sects, though there is more agreement in essentials than there is between the divisions of most other religions. There are three principal groups, the "Orthodox," the Roman Catholic, and the Protestant, the latter including a number of smaller divisions or "denominations." It may not be unfair to think of them as being differentiated by race almost as much as by creed and practice. The first group, it is true, includes several large divisions, all of which recognize one another. They are the Eastern (including the ancient Church of southern India), the African (i.e. Egyptian and Abyssinian), and the Greek, of which the largest national group is the Russian. Whilst recognizing one another, these look to different episcopal sees for the source of their orders and for their supreme authority. The Roman Catholic Church is essentially the Christianity of the Latin peoples of the western Mediterranean, though it is also the predominant form of Christianity in Ireland and in southern Germany, while Protestantism may be described as the interpretation of Christianity by the Teutonic races of north-western Europe.

The differences in formal doctrine between the Orthodox and the Roman Catholic Churches are comparatively slight. In practice, however, there are wider variations. In the Roman Church, for instance, all beneficed clergy must be celibate, whether they are in monastic orders or not, whilst in the Orthodox Church those who are engaged in parochial work must be married, though they are

M*

debarred from the higher offices. The most striking difference, however, is to be found in the administration of the Eucharist or "Mass," for the Roman Catholic Church allows the laity to partake of the bread only, the wine being reserved for the clergy, whilst in the Orthodox Church both elements are received by the laity. Further, in the Orthodox Church the elements may be administered to infants immediately after baptism, whilst the Roman Church "communion" is postponed till adolescence, though not necessarily till after "confirmation." Another interesting point of difference is that, whilst in the Orthodox Church worship may be conducted in the vernacular, the Roman Catholic service is normally read in Latin.

Protestantism arose in the sixteenth century in different parts of northern Europe, almost spontaneously and simultaneously. There are, therefore, marked differences between the various forms that this type of Christianity takes. All agree, however, in repudiating the direct authority of the Bishop of Rome, and none insists on the practice of confession to a priest, though it would not be true to say that confession is excluded from all Protestant communities. Worship is always conducted in the vernacular, and the Communion is administered to the laity in both kinds. For the most part, also, Protestants reject the doctrine of Purgatory. Apart from these points there is little on which all bodies of Protestants would agree as against the Orthodox and Roman Catholic Churches, but in actual practice there is a large measure of harmony between them; they normally respect one another, and are prepared to work together.

The Christian ethic has two sides; one of these we may call personal, the other social. As a practical guide to external conduct, the standard of the higher Judaism is generally accepted, especially as it finds expression in the so-called "Decalogue." Thus theft, murder, fornication, and falsehood are generally recognized as inconsistent with a profession of Christianity, and usually slothfulness, drunkenness, and other forms of misconduct are condemned. But Christian morality is far from being a series of prohibitions; it not merely forbids certain acts, but it enjoins a spirit and an outlook. It is usual to refer to the so-called "Sermon on the Mount" (Matt. v-vii) as the truest statement of the Christian ethic. But it must be remembered that this discourse offers only a series of illustrations of the teaching of Jesus, and that they need to be related to fundamental principles. Too close an attention to details may give the impression that the Christian ethic is a casuistic system of conduct, a dictionary of life to which the inquirer can turn in case of doubt and find the exact circumstances and the exact prescription to meet his need. In the ethic of Jesus the stress is necessarily laid on essential principles, of which the rest of the instruction is to be regarded as illustration, much of it due to temporary conditions and to circumstances which no longer exist.

Probably the centre of the moral teaching on the personal side is to be found in the doctrine of self-denial. This does not involve asceticism or active renunciation of pleasure or luxury; it goes deeper than such expedients for avoiding selfishness. To "deny" is to refuse to recognize at all, to shut out of thought and consideration, to disown. A man who denies himself, therefore, is one who refuses to consider or to recognize his own needs, wishes, ambitions, and desires. When he is calculating the arguments for a particular course of action, the last thing that must enter his mind is his own personal interest. This, of course, does not exclude the need for the recognition of his own powers and capabilities, or the demand made on him to keep himself in a state of efficiency, but he must think of and treat himself from a purely impersonal point of view, and while he has no right to waste his powers or to allow them to deteriorate, he must be ready, at the call of that to which he is devoted, on the claim of anything in which he recognizes the voice of God, to risk and surrender everything.

It is only through this complete self-abnegation, says Jesus, that true self-realization can be obtained. "He who loves himself will ruin himself, but he who ruins himself . . . will preserve himself." Here is the great paradox of Christian ethics, that a man becomes of value to God and his fellows only when he has ceased to place any value on himself at all. He holds life and all else on the same tenure as a soldier in time of war, and his function can only be fulfilled if he is ready to throw himself away at need. It should be observed that there is little emphasis on sacrifice or suffering for its own sake; such considerations may lead to a rarefied and subtle, yet very deadly, form of selfishness.

It is obvious that such a doctrine can be valid only if there is presented some object in whose interests the surrender is made. In the teaching of Jesus this appears in a double form, the final object being God Himself, and the nearer one the Christian's fellow men. For the Christian ethic is a corollary of the Christian experience. Jesus laid down no laws of conduct for the outside world; He never preached righteousness to those whom his contemporaries called sinners. He recognized that they were sinners, yet, as far as we know, He made no attempt to condemn them, but rather defended them against the professional moralists of His day. His instructions for life were offered to His own disciples, those who had accepted Him as their leader and guide, and were prepared to recognize His authority as supreme. His first requirement was one of personal allegiance; that assured, He could proceed to direct the course of their lives, but He could deal only with men and women who had made the initial act of consecration. This fact is, perhaps, insufficiently recognized, and Christian moralists have too often assumed that the standard of life set by Jesus should be imposed on all alike, irrespective of their personal adherence to God in Christ.

From the experience of faith, then, the rest follows. A moral union with God, a mystical surrender to God, will mean that he who is thus consecrated and lost in God will exhibit the character of God, in so far as he understands it, in his dealings with men. God is a universal Father; from this it follows that all men are brothers, and that no distinctions can be drawn between them which fail to give due weight to the claims of personality. This is summed up in what we commonly call "the Golden Rule": "Whatsoever ye would that men should do unto you, so do ye also unto them," rightly accepted as an ideal guide for conduct. But the instructions of Jesus go far below conduct, and search out the motives and thoughts that lie behind speech and action. To Him the right and the wrong lie, not in the deeds, but in the state of mind and soul which produce them, and His constant demand is for a change which shall go to the roots of personality.

For the moral standard of Jesus does not derive its supreme value merely from the type of conduct which it inculcates. Parallels may be found elsewhere; the Stoic, the Pharisee, the Confucian, and the Buddhist would all offer similar ideals, and comparisons with one or all of these forms of teaching are sometimes quoted. But this difference is to be observed: the ethic of the first three named, and perhaps also of the last, is essentially a morality of repression. It finds that there are certain instincts and tendencies lying deep below the surface in human nature, whose natural expression will lead to wrong done to a man's fellows. The only way to secure a good and helpful mode of life is to repress these instincts and to hold them in check, to drive them below the surface so that they may not appear in outward conduct. Hence the feeling—particularly obvious in the Stoic and the Pharisee —that to be a good man was a task for a professional, that it would take a man's whole time and attention, and that it must be his first interest in life. Jesus, on the other hand, demanded a morality of expression, one which should give free course to all human instinct, though not in its crude shape but in a "sublimated" form. The good man, in His judgement, did good because his nature had been changed, and he did it unconsciously, not knowing that it was good, but simply because it seemed to him the "natural" and obvious thing to do. Change the heart, turn all instinct Godwards, and they can be trusted to work out a proper mode of life without having rules imposed on it from above and consciously accepted as canons of life. It is a signficant fact that Paul of Tarsus himself had been a Pharisee, and had found that, in spite of his best efforts, the Pharisaic morality failed to give him what he needed. This he found only in the ethic that sprang from his own faith, his mystic union with and surrender to Christ. It has frequently been observed that the early Church was persecuted often by those who set before them standards of conduct similar to its own, and this must be explained in part as due to the jealousy of the professional for the amateur, of the man who had laboriously attained to his high position for him who reached it spontaneously and without effort.

The social ethic of Jesus may perhaps best be summed up in the phrase "Kingdom of God"—or, as it may perhaps better be rendered, "Kingship of God." The exact meaning of the term has been disputed, and there has been and still is a tendency to interpret it in an eschatological sense. Historically there is much to justify this view, and it may well be that it was the thought uppermost in the minds of those who heard Jesus use the words. But a close study of His own references to the Kingdom of God makes it clear that this element, if present at all, occupied a subordinate place in His own thinking. It rather implies the absolute, unchallenged, and unconditioned dominance of the Will of God in all things human. It is a social as well as an individual ideal, and it is clear that Jesus contemplated the existence of a form of society which should give it expression. Within that society the primary demand made on each member was that of service to the whole. Pre-eminence amongst His followers was to be secured, not by the amount of attention and obedience they received from others, but by the extent to which they subordinated themselves to the interests of the whole community. Jesus created no special political order, but rather laid the stress on the equal responsibility of everyone of His followers for the attainment of His ideal throughout the world. That God should be not only Father but also King—and the connotation of that term to the Eastern mind always includes unlimited authority—over all humanity was the object for which each and all must strive. Important as the individual was, the whole body was more important still, and demanded all the energies of the consecrated life. To this day every Christian repeats, in the one universal form of prayer used by all Churches and bodies, the words enjoined by Jesus, "Our Father which art in Heaven, hallowed be Thy name. Thy Kingdom come; Thy will be done in earth as it is in Heaven."

# BIBLIOGRAPHY

IT is obviously impossible to offer a comprehensive bibliography of so vast a subject, or even an extensive selection. But it is hoped that the following brief list may help the student to follow up any line of special interest. Each book may suggest others which, for one reason or another, are not included below.

## I. GENERAL

Among books which deal with the whole field, attention may be called to the following: A. C. Bouquet, *Comparative Religion*; Estlin Carpenter, *Comparative Religion*; L. R. Farnell, *The Evolution of Religion*; E. O. James, *Comparative Religion*; N. Micklem, *Religion*. H. Smith, *The Elements of Comparative Theology*. N. Söderblom, *The Living God*. As a very simple factual statement, W. Paton, *Jesus Christ and the World's Religions*, may be recommended. Special studies in Sacrifice are contained in G. B. Gray, *Sacrifice in the Old Testament*; E. O. James, *The Origins of Sacrifice*; W. O. E. Oesterley, *Sacrifices in Ancient Israel*; W. Robertson Smith, *Religion of the Semites* (3rd Ed.). There are also numerous articles by experts in the *Encyclopædia of Religion and Ethics*.

## II AND III. PROTO-RELIGION AND ANIMISM

Most of the works which deal with the early stages of religion are general studies in the life of "primitive" peoples. The great corpus of material is J. G. Frazer's *Golden Bough*. More concentrated studies will be found in E. O. James, *Primitive Religion and Belief* and *The Beginnings of Religion*; R. Karsten, *Origins of Religion*; Levy-Bruhl, *Primitives and the Supernatural*; B. Malinowski, *The Foundations of Faith and Morals*; R. R. Marrett, *The Threshold of Religion* and *Anthropology*; R. Otto, *The Idea of the Holy*; P. Radin, *Primitive Religion*; G. Roheim, *Animism, Magic, and the Divine Being*; W. Schmidt, *The Origin and Growth of Religion*; E. B. Tylor, *Primitive Culture*; E. Waterhouse, *The Dawn of Religion* (a very simple and clear statement). We have also numbers of works dealing with limited fields, such as G. Barton, *A Study of Semitic Origins*; J. Harrison, *Prolegomena to the Study of Greek Religion*; R. R. Marrett, *Argonauts of the Western Pacific*; W. O. E. Oesterley, *Immortality and the Unseen World*; W. H. R. Rivers, *The Todas*; J. Roscoe, *The Baganda*; E. Smith, *The Ila-speaking Peoples of Northern Rhodesia*; B. Spencer and F. J. Gillen, *Native Tribes of Central Australia* and *Northern Tribes of Central Australia*.

## IV. POLYTHEISM

There are many monographs on the great Polytheisms. The following may be suggested, in addition to such texts as are translated in *The Sacred Books of the East:*

BABYLONIA: M. Jastrow, *Religion of Babylonia and Assyria; Religious Belief in Babylonia and Assyria.*

EGYPT: J. H. Breasted, *Development of Religion and Thought in Ancient Egypt*; Wallis Budge, *Tutankhamen*; A. Erman, *A Handbook of Egyptian Religion*; A. W. Shorter, *An Introduction to Egyptian Religion.*

GREECE AND ROME: S. Angus, *The Mystery Religions and Christianity*; A. B. Cook, *Zeus*; W. W. Fowler,

*Religious Experience of the Roman People; Roman Ideas of Deity*; G. Murray, *Five Stages of Greek Religion*; M. P. Nilson, *A History of Greek Religion*; H. J. Rose, *Ancient Greek Religion* and *Ancient Roman Religion*.

INDIA (HINDU): L. D. Barnett, *Hindu Gods and Heroes*; S. Cave, *Living Religions of the East*; C. Eliot, *Hinduism and Buddhism*; J. N. Farquhar, *Primer of Hinduism; The Crown of Hinduism* and *Outline of the Religious Literature of India*; A. B. Keith, *Religion and Philosophy of the Vedas and Upanishads*; E. A. Payne, *The Saktas*; Monier Williams, *Brahmanism and Hinduism*.

JAPAN: D. C. Holtom, *The National Faith of Japan*; A. C. Underwood, *Shintoism*.

# V. AND VI. PHILOSOPHY AND RELIGION; PHILOSOPHICAL RELIGIONS

The classical work on Indian philosophy is P. Deussen, *The Philosophy of the Upanishads*. Also to be noted are Estlin Carpenter, *Theism in Modern India*; R. E. Hume, *The Thirteen Principal Upanishads*; W. S. Urquhart, *The Vedanta and Modern Thought*. Most of the books mentioned under Hinduism contain sketches of the main schools of thought. There are more specialized studies such as J. N. Rawson, *The Katha Upanishad*, and an Indian point of view is presented by Kirayauna, *Outlines of Indian Philosophy* and Radhakrishnan, *Indian Philosophy*.

For Buddhism in general the student may be referred to T. W. Rhys Davids, *A Manual of Buddhism* and *Outlines of Buddhism*. More specialised treatment may be found in C. Eliot, *Japanese Buddhism*; L. Hodous, *Buddhism and Buddhists in China*; K. Saunders, *The Heart of Buddhism* and *Epochs in Buddhist History* (both useful for the *Mahayana* in its modern form); Steiner-Oberlin, *The Buddhist Sects of Japan*.

Among works in Chinese religion and Confucianism may be mentioned H. A. Giles, *Confucianism and its Rivals*; J. Legge, *The Religions of China*; W. E. Soothill, *The Three Religions of China*.

## VII. MONOTHEISM

For Zoroastrianism see especially J. H. Moulton, *Early Zoroastrianism* and *The Treasure of the Magi*. The latter book includes a study of modern Parsiism. A sketch of the traditional life of Zoroaster may be found in A. V. W. Jackson, *Zoroaster: the Prophet of Ancient Iran*.

Among the numerous books on the religion of Israel the following may be noted: W. F. Albright, *From the Stone Age to Christianity* and *Archæology and the Religion of Israel*; A. Lods, *Israel*; W. O. E. Oesterley and T. H. Robinson, *Hebrew Religion*; J. Pedersen, *Israel*; H. W. Robinson, *Religious Ideas of the Old Testament* and *The Old Testament: its Making and Meaning*; J. N. Schofield, *The Religious Background of the Old Testament*.

## VIII. ISLAM

There are several English translations of the Qur'an, especially those of J. M. Rodwell and R. Bell; the latter arranges the Suras in chronological order. Reference may be made to articles in *The Encyclopædia of Islam*, and a Moslem, sometimes anti-Christian view is presented by Ameer Ali, *The Spirit of Islam*. Other books include S. Cave, *Living Religions of the East*; H. A. R. Gibb, *Mohammedanism*; L. B. Jones, *The People of the Mosque* and *Woman in Islam*; D. M. Kay, *The Semitic Religions*; D. B. MacDonald, *Muslim Theology*; D. S. Margoliouth, *Mohammed and the Rise of Islam* and *Early Development of Islam*; R. A. Nicholson, *Islamic Mysticism*; J. W. Sweetman, *Islam and Christian Theology*.

## IX. CHRISTIANITY

It should be unnecessary to specify books on Christianity for the guidance of the student, but a study of its relation to other religions may be found in H. Kraemar, *The Christian Message in a Non-Christian World*; W. E. Hocking, *Living Religions and a World Faith*.

# INDEX